YOU and Your Own Universe

Silviu Pristavu

ISBN: 979-8-4468-0585-3

CONTENTS

Preface   1

Chapter 1 What If …?   7

Chapter 2 Conscious and Subconscious   13

Chapter 3 Purpose   51

Chapter 4 Thoughts, Emotions, and Feelings   64

Chapter 5 Belief   105

Chapter 6 Universal Consciousness   130

Chapter 7 The Power of Action   158

Chapter 8 Habits   185

Chapter 9 Relationships   194

Chapter 10 Health   210

Chapter 11 Show Me the Money   222

Chapter 12 The I in You   244

Acknowledgments   255

References   256

PREFACE

This book is not religious! It doesn't aim to favor one religion or discredit another. If anything, it's a tool for any religion that's been created from the beginning of humanity and helps explain phenomena that couldn't have been explained otherwise. It supports science equally; however, it doesn't just support theories that are based purely on physical evidence, though it may provide answers where these haven't been found yet, if one is open to accepting a different point of view. It was written to serve as a manual for life, explaining how things become what they are and providing confidence and strength to teens getting ready to face the world on their own, and to adults who feel lost, without a purpose, and in need of guidance toward a happy life.

Think about your smartphone. It wouldn't have been possible if it wasn't for the existence of a wired phone, a computer, and the internet. The wired phone wouldn't have existed if it wasn't for Alexander Graham Bell. In the beginning, the computer was as big as an entire room. Wireless internet wouldn't have been possible without the marvelous discovery of Marconi. Think about all the components of your smartphone and realize that each and every one of them is the highest form of evolution of its previous forms. This book is not my invention; this book is the result of the work of hundreds and thousands of people throughout history. Their work from the beginning of writing to this day has been reshaped and reformed in the light of new information discovered century by century. I'm only building on the work of millions of people since the beginning of the world – to whom I am truly grateful.

A study was carried out to test whether the relationship between exercise and health is moderated by one's mindset. In a group of hotels, 84 female room attendants were divided into two parts by Alia J. Crum and Ellen J. Langer from Harvard University, who made sure there was no possible interaction between the two parts. One half were invited, one by one, and told that they were going to be part of a study and measurements would be taken of their body functions, e.g. heart rate, blood pressure, BMI, etc. After that, they were informed of the implications of their work – walking up and down the stairs, hoovering, cleaning, and so on – and how this work helps their body's health in a positive way. The other half were informed only of the fact they were part of the study; their measurements were taken, but no other information was given.

Four weeks later, new measurements were taken from the two groups. The results were this: the group who weren't given any details of the study, and weren't made aware of the implications of their work, recorded more or less the same figures. The first group, who were made aware of how their work improves their health, had registered decrease in weight, blood pressure, body fat, waist-to-hip ratio and BMI, a much healthier condition overall. (Crum and Langer, 2007)

The conclusion is that just the awareness of new information can make our brain transform our body and through it our entire lifestyle. Whenever you think, interact, create, or imagine, if you keep the idea you'll discover in this book in the back of your mind, your life will start to flourish in ways you can't imagine right now, and when you look back and see how much it's changed your future, you will be grateful for having dedicated the few hours required to read this book. If you go beyond that and look deeper into studying and applying the idea into your life, great wealth, pure health, and abundant happiness will pour out of you and fill your life and the lives of those who are connected with you.

Bruce Lee said, "Empty your cup so that it may be filled; become devoid to gain totality." In other words, in order to learn something new, we first have to unlearn what we already know. For the content of this book, to pierce through years of knowledge that you have collected from your peers, school, society, media, etc., you must open your mind. Let go of all you know, let go of the resistance of your mind to judge the content of this book, and embrace the possibility of a higher potential.

Through the ages, humanity has relied too much upon its physical sense, and has limited its knowledge to the physical things – what we see, touch, weigh, and measure – this has limited our living potential. When we encounter people who discover a way to break through this limited barrier set by the mind, and allow themselves to express freely in the physical world through methods that seem like miracles, our mind first judges them and then discredits them before accepting them for what they really are.

The mind, in its limited ways, knows nothing of this amazing power that's within you. It tries to explain the unseen with the seen, the incomparable by comparing it with what it can perceive through its five senses. And as you can see so far, it hasn't succeeded yet; we're still in the dark and call certain things miracles.

Chapter 1

WHAT IF…?

What if you found out that you're not who you believe you are? What if I told you that you're not who your family thinks you are? What if you're not the person that people around you see and hear …

What if the human being is, in reality, the fusing element of two worlds – physical and spiritual? What if, in the human body, you can find both physical and spiritual, where the spiritual manifests physically. What if what we call the mind, as we know it, is actually the gate through which the two worlds meet, cross, and exchange information? What You are, as a spiritual being, can't be described in any human language.

What You are can't be seen by any human eyes. What You say can't be heard by any physical ears. You are something that can only be felt through your physical body, and you will feel You long before you finish reading this book.

You are not your body. The body has been given to you, or probably you've earned it, or even created it yourself. Probably, it's just a vehicle for You to ride in through this life. Your body is in a constant transformation, as proven by science, through the creation of millions of cells daily, but not You, because You are perfect just the way You are. You never say, "I am this body," or "I am my arm," or "I am my head." You say, "I have a body," "I have a head," etc. "I have" means that you possess it, not that you identify with it.

You are not your mind. The mind is the software of your brain. If we were to compare the human body with an android – a robot with a human appearance – the android needs, in broad terms, hardware, a memory drive, and software to operate, or artificial intelligence. If the hardware breaks, the software doesn't work properly or at all. Similarly, in the human body, if the brain dies, the mind doesn't work anymore.

You are not your name. Your name was given to you when you were born, but you are not it. You are not stuck with it either. You can change your name, but you can't change who You are; the name is given to your body. Young children don't identify with their body or their given name until later on, when the mind takes control. If you show two-year-old Anastasia a picture of herself, she will say, "That's Anastasia"; she won't say, "That's me."

You are a spiritual being living in a human body. You are the awareness in you – the consciousness. You are the love, the joy, and the happiness that bursts out of you. You are the creator of your body and the creator of Your Own Universe. You are limitless. You are wealth. You are health. You are all these things combined and more.

Throughout time people have tried to answer two questions: "Where have we come from?" and "Where are we going?" The only reason these questions are still unanswered is because we've asked them from a limited perception – from the perception of our mind. It's true that our DNA is capable of storing massive amounts of information. It's true that this information is also transferred through generations from ancestors to descendants. And it's also true that with every generation we keep on adding more information to our DNA. But no matter how much information we add, there is still more to add, and we've only tried answering these questions from a limited perspective – from the limited experience of our mind and body transformed from one generation to another.

"If the human brain were a computer, it would perform thirty-eight thousand trillion operations per second;" this is how powerful the human brain is, and You created that! "The world's most powerful supercomputer, Blue-Gene, can manage only 0.002% of that." (Kellett, 2014). That is what the human mind managed to create so far.

And even though we keep adding more information every day into the memory of our brain, there is always going to be more information to be added, and the way our mind executes commands and draws conclusions will always be limited to the amount of information stored.

We are aware, in our mind, that there is something within us that is bigger than the limitations of our body. This something has been given many names throughout history and time: the inner self, the higher self, the guardian angel, the sixth sense, the soul, etc. These are but names given by our limited mind to the beings that we are, but we are beyond our mind's capability to describe ourselves. It's like asking Siri, Cortana, or Alexa to describe you – your feelings and emotions, your drive and motivation – the answer will be limited, general, and also a funny one. For the rest of the book, I will call this being You.

From the mind's perspective, the attributes that You bring into play, which the mind can't explain, are all classed under a generic term – the sixth sense. The mind knows of its five senses: sight, hearing, touch, taste, and smell, and has classed Your manifestation into the physical world not as a user or an entity (the mind assumes it has all the power over the body) but as a sixth sense, because it hasn't been educated to be what it's supposed to be – a servant for You. According to the mind, the sixth sense is responsible for premonitions, clairvoyance, gut feeling, hunches, telepathy, and any other inexplicable "hints" or "tips."

Napoleon Hill is one of the greatest people known in the personal development industry, and one who studied over 500 successful people in America in the early 1900s. In his iconic book, *Think and Grow Rich*, he describes You like this:

> The sixth sense defies description! It can't be described to a person [...] Understanding of the sixth sense comes only by meditation through mind development from within. The sixth sense probably is the medium of contact between the finite mind of man and Infinite Intelligence, and for this reason, it's a mixture of both the mental and the spiritual. It's believed to be the point at which the human mind contacts the Universal Mind [...] the fact remains that human beings do receive accurate knowledge, through sources other than the physical senses. (Hill, 2007)

Your mind is your best friend because your mind is with you everywhere you go. It shares all the memories of your body, all your experiences, and everything else, but it doesn't know who you truly are until You reveal yourself to it. It thinks of You as "the voice inside my head," the trustworthy friend who gives it a nudge every now and then, but what if the mind is actually the voice You hear?

Reveal yourself to your mind for who You really are by raising the awareness of yourself and realizing You are not your mind and You are not your body – You are the pure infinite being that came to this physical world to experience the beauty of creation.

Throughout the ages, people have used the practice of meditation to connect with the divine, the infinite, to find peace and true purpose. If you've meditated before, you know that already. Use meditation as a tool to raise awareness inside your mind about You. Elevate your mind by revealing yourself to it, providing it with the faith that its best friend, its master, is its creator.

Chapter 2

CONSCIOUS AND SUBCONSCIOUS

For as long as we can remember, the conscious and subconscious have both been attributed to the mind like two sides of the same coin, two ends of the same stick, or two halves of the same sphere. Whether they've been called objective and subjective, awake and asleep, voluntary and involuntary, or even male and female; it was done so because we always looked at things and tried to explain the mind from the same perspective – the mind's perspective. We assume that if the brain that holds the mind is physical, the mind, both conscious and subconscious, must be from this world too, but remember that we concluded this with our minds.

The voice inside your head – that is the voice of your mind! Many struggle to see the difference between the good voice and the "wrong" one. For instance, when you're in doubt and don't know what to do, and this voice in your head hints to you – sometimes you go right, but sometimes you go wrong, which then creates that forever doubt and makes you question every decision you have to make. Well, that voice is the voice of your mind and it comes from rationalizing. You, on the other hand, manifest your will, not through logic, not through words or images, but through feelings in your whole body.

You, the being, don't have a vocabulary, per se, to express yourself through words. Words are for the mind to communicate with other humans and are limited to the communities they live in or the number of speakers of that language. The mind can learn one language or seven, it's just something that the mind is capable of, while You have a different kind of communication system in place. You can literally communicate with any human being on the planet regardless of whether you share a common language or not.

Go to any country in the world and you will be able to communicate with any human being if you let go of the language barrier; you will find a way to express yourself and understand the locals without the need to understand their language. When you're unable to communicate physically, another form of communication arises from within – like a person who loses their sight and all the other senses are increased. It's the same when your ability to express through words doesn't get through to another, the You opens a bridge from within. Moreover, it isn't limited strictly to humans; it applies to animals and plants as well.

This form of communication is through your feelings, and it works only when you let go of the mind, open your heart, and allow You to take the lead. If you follow "your heart" when in doubt, you can never go wrong! If you have a tough decision to make and the voice in your head tells you something but you're struggling to accept it, ask yourself "What feels good right now?" Forget about logic; that's limited to your mind's memory and its capacity to process the information stored. Follow your good feelings, because that is the core of your being – that is the way You communicate with yourself.

"Consciousness," said Neville Goddard (2015), "is the one and only reality, not figuratively, but actually."

We know for a fact that the human body is a mass of energy. "You have enough potential power in your body to illuminate the whole city in which you live for nearly a week." (Proctor, 2016). But what happens with all that energy when the heart stops beating? Or when You leaves the body? What if, in reality, the heart stops beating because You leaves the body? There is no more energy in the body, and that's why the body starts to disintegrate. Could it be that this "energy" is what keeps the body alive? The "consciousness" ceases to exist. There is still some neurological activity in the brain, the subconsciousness, but no consciousness.

Assuming that this energy is what keeps life in the body, the following statement should be true:

Consciousness is the energy manifesting in the body – You.

Subconscious is the programming that manifests the body and its actions – the mind.

> The law of your mind is this: You get a reaction or response from your subconscious mind according to the nature of the thought or idea you hold in your conscious mind. (Murphy, 2011, p. 8)

You are the master, and your mind is the servant. You command the servant. You set the routines. You dictate the time for dinner and the time of sleep, when you should enjoy yourself and when you should go to work. Your mind is there to help You and support You, and to do all the physical chores for You. Yes, You have to show it how to do it in the first place (if you want it done properly), but then you let it be, to carry on with its programming.

Walking, running, riding, writing, and reading are all habits that your mind couldn't master at some point, but with Your perseverance and motivation, You taught your mind to do them, and they're all done by default now. If You want to change the way your body walks one time, you can do so, and You can retrain your mind to do it like that whenever you want; if You want to change your handwriting style, you can do so, and You can retrain your mind to do it like that more often; if You want to create a habit of exercising at a certain point of the day, You can train your mind to do it; or if You want to wake up at a certain time, You can train your mind to do it. If You want to start smoking, You can train your mind to do it, and if You want to quit smoking, You can train your mind to do that, too.

> Through the ages, humanity has depended too much upon its physical sense, and has limited its knowledge to physical things, which we could see, touch, weight, and measure. (Hill, 2007)

The mind isn't in charge of your body – You are! The mind doesn't like change; it "knows" that everything You taught it is "the truth" and that's its law. The mind only resists change because it's the best servant and it obeys the truth. As a child, you borrowed the truth from parents, tutors, neighbors, educators, teachers, government, religion, etc. Now, You are your own master and can decide a new truth – your truth! And if the new truth doesn't serve you well, You can change it again, and again, and again, until the truth that You decide is the truth that serves You best.

Your mind's programming, or paradigm, is a cumulation of habits, truths that You gave your (subconscious) mind to execute. At the time those truths were agreed upon, they were "the best truth" You discovered. Before America was discovered, people believed the earth to be flat – that was their truth. Columbus had a different truth, and he sailed toward the "edge" of the earth with no fear of "falling off," as his contemporary fellows believed. Magellan confirmed this truth years later sailing around the globe. When news spread, people started changing their truth, changed their belief, and changed their mind's programming.

The mind's thinking is independent and based exclusively on the facts or truths that are stored in its memory. As a child, you had a different truth from an adult – it was mostly based on the intuition of You. As you've grown and learned the ways of the people you met, your mind's truth adapted. As you travel, explore, and read, new information gets stored in your mind and new truths are born.

> Your mind is an instrument, a tool. It is there to be used for a specific task, and when the task is completed, you lay it down. As it is, I would say about 80 to 90 percent of most people's thinking is not only repetitive and useless, but because of its dysfunctional and often negative nature, much of it is also harmful. Observe your mind and you will find this to be true. It causes a serious leakage of vital energy. This kind of compulsive thinking is actually an addiction. What characterizes an addiction? Quite simply this: you no longer feel that you have the choice to stop. It seems stronger than you. It also gives you a false sense of pleasure, pleasure that invariably turns into pain. (Tolle, 2000)

Allowing the mind to do the thinking for you leads to addiction, like Eckhart Tolle mentioned above. Relying on your mind's thinking is, frankly, being lazy. Most people refuse to believe that they're the creators of their own universe simply because they don't feel in control of their own thoughts – their mind is doing all the thinking. They feel powerless in controlling their thoughts; therefore, they're powerless in controlling the outcome of their own life, blame others for adversity, and rely on luck, or fortunes.

Your power and knowledge come from the "universal consciousness." Some call it God, some Allah, some call it Brahma, or Shangdi, and others simply the universe.

It doesn't matter what name our mind decided to give to the source of its master; what matters is that there is one, without which nothing would be in existence as we know it. Silencing your mind's thoughts allows you to have a stronger connection with the universal consciousness where you can download information that doesn't exist in your mind's memory; therefore, giving You the ability to make wiser choices.

The mind evolves, learns, and grows with the help of the five senses, and it controls the body. It's designed to create little programs which we call habits, and is also designed to execute commands, or to follow instructions, but not to lead. There are billions of "followers" on this planet because they allow their mind to take charge of their lives. When any of these people hit that level we call "rock-bottom," their mind crashes. It can't figure a way out, so it shuts down. That's when You wakes up. Those who stay in this awakening reach high peaks and become great leaders of the world, and stories "from rags to riches" are born.

However, there are still a few who, once recovered from the collapse, get back to their "usual" life and hand over, once again, the daily life to their lieutenant – the mind. The purpose of this book is to make You aware of your power. You have an extraordinary lieutenant willing to go above and beyond for You and follow any instructions for the benefit of your wellbeing. However, this lieutenant is very eager to assume command with every opportunity. Once we hand over the full command to an inexperienced lieutenant, we have to accept the results as well – good or bad.

Those who identify themselves with their mind find it very hard to accept their mistakes, though they aren't actually their mistakes. They are results of the actions of an inexperienced lieutenant. Their only mistake was to hand over command before properly training their lieutenant, and that can easily be rectified. When You separate yourself from your mind, You can objectively see the difference between your actions and the actions of your mind. You are proactive, while your mind is reactive. You are creative, while your mind is repetitive. You are strong, while your mind is weak. You are love, while your mind is fear.

We could also compare the mind with a garden in which seeds (ideas) are planted to grow and multiply. The seeds can be flowers, fruits, vegetables, or even weeds. For the untrained mind, a seed doesn't say much about what it could become if planted in the garden, but as you look after the garden and pay attention to all the details, you get to know your seeds. Ideas are the same. A child gets all sorts of ideas, which in the unformed mind, they will have no clue of what they will become, until they spring out and bloom. Sometimes it's something that impresses their parents, while other times it could turn into an accident. Only after we have seen the flower of the seed planted can we decide whether to plant that seed again in the future or not.

Throughout our childhood many of our ideas have been crushed, even before we had the chance to plant them in our garden. This, too, transformed into a habit – the habit of killing off ideas before we planted them. How do you know if your idea, the seed that you just found, will be a beautiful flower or not? Why kill it? Because others think it's not worth it? Because others say, "Nobody ever planted such a seed before"? Why would You allow the minds of others to dictate what you plant in your own garden? Why would You grow a garden that looks the same as your neighbor's?

Whenever you find a new seed, a new idea that springs to mind, go ahead and plant it. Do it in a corner where no one else can see it if you're afraid of judgement. When that idea starts to bloom, both you and your neighbors will be able to see its true form.

When Henry Ford built his first car, people judged it and labelled it in discouraging ways saying, "Nobody will pay money for such a hideous thing." The fact that today there are five new cars produced every two seconds (Worldometer) is proof that his seed was worth planting.

When the Wright Brothers, two bicycle mechanics, came up with the idea of building a plane, people laughed at them and their idea, and told them they were wasting their time because nobody had done it before. In the last twenty-four hours alone, over 150,000 planes took off (flightradar24.com), which is proof that their idea was a seed worth planting.

> It may interest you to know that Marconi's friends had him taken into custody and examined in a psychopathic hospital, when he announced he had discovered the principle through which he could send messages through the air, without the aid of wires or other direct physical means of communication. (Hill, 2007).

Look around you. Radio, TV, Internet, and mobile phones – all wireless. Nobody calls him insane now!

I'm not saying that all your ideas will change the world as we know it, I'm saying that any of your ideas change Your world as You know it, and by your example and leadership, the rest of the world may also change. The more you trust your ideas and have faith in them, the more encouragement will come to bring about new ideas, explore new possibilities, and live the life You have on this earth on multiple levels.

It may be hard for our minds to grasp the majestic power that we have, as beings on this earth, and refusing to believe in this power doesn't change a thing – we are still activating it, just not to our liking.

Remember – You are love, and joy, and peace. **You are not your mind!**

Don't be afraid to be what You are and what you want to be. Actually, fear isn't even one of Your feelings. It may feel like one, but it's just our mind's defensive system creating scenarios and releasing adrenaline and other chemicals into our body to protect itself. Your mind has no way of protecting You; a physical creation, your creation nonetheless, can't comprehend that You are in no danger in the physical world, that You are safe no matter what, and that this life on Earth for You is just a journey.

If you like the idea of going on vacation to different places that you can visit, discover, and enjoy, think of You in this world just like that – your journey to a vacation. What are you doing on your journey? Get in a car, a plane, or a train and explore. That's the body for You – a means of transportation that You use to explore and experience this wonderful life on Earth.

Depending on Your destination, You picks a certain means of transportation. Sometimes it's a European body, while other times it's African or Asian. Sometimes it's broken when you get it, while other times it breaks down. Think of it as a choice, not as luck. Imagine that You picked your body intentionally for the experience, and explore all you can in your body – make the most of it; You only have it once.

Most probably we'll never be able to perceive with our minds the main destination of our journey, but we will always "feel" the direction we're heading, and as long as we follow our heart, the inspiration, we will reach our destination. Only when we rely on our mind for directions, we get lost, confused, and ready to give up. Don't confuse Your up-to-date navigation system with the one of your mind. Your mind's navigation system is created as it evolves, and as NASA's Rover on Mars, it first explores, discovers, and then maps out. It's never complete, continuously improving with the new discoveries, and more than often you'll find yourself in some sort of dead end, or cul-de-sac.

On the other hand, Your navigation system is like a satellite that has eyes above and knows the way before you reach it. The most beautiful part is that it sends you tips and information about your journey ahead, similar to a Google navigation system, and sends you information about traffic, accidents, or things that you are about to encounter on your journey. Some call these signals premonitions, divine inspirations, guardian angels, etc. It doesn't really matter what you call them, what we can all agree on is that they manifest through feelings, often described as "gut feelings." You feel when something isn't "right", though your mind will question that feeling and try to rationalize it. Your feeling is always the right call.

Successful people always say, "Never give up," "Keep trying," "A quitter never wins, and a winner never quits," or "Be perseverant" because they understand this principle. They understand that hitting a dead end is nothing but the result of using an incomplete map, and the same way you try to find your way out of a maze, you have to keep on searching for the right exit, and the more you learn from mistakes, from dead ends, the faster you reach your destination. They're teaching you how to train your mind to reach a destination.

Thomas A. Edison is one of the most iconic figures in the history of humanity known for his perseverance. When asked how he felt about failing so many times trying to prove the idea of the light bulb, he said, "I have not failed. I've just found 10,000 ways that won't work." (AZ Quotes). Though, it was only when he gave up trying to use his limited mind that he connected to "the source" – the universal consciousness – and materialized his vision.

The body is the bridge connection between the invisible, or spiritual world, and the visible, or physical world. The spiritual world is invisible to the mind; it can't be seen with the five senses, with which the mind can only perceive the physical world, but through the body you can feel the non-physical world.

You can only perceive the physical world with your body, but You are always connected to the invisible world. Telepathy, gut feeling, inspiration, and thought impulse are all "senses" of the spirit/energy. These are the communication methods used to transcend the two worlds.

Thoughts

There are two types of thoughts: the ones that your mind creates and that you can observe running in the background like a radio or a TV – to which you pay little or no attention – and the ones that You intentionally plant in your mind. You can call them conscious and unconscious thoughts. Either way, whether conscious or unconscious, they're still seeds of creation that give shape and form to the images that show up on the screen of your mind.

> The subconscious mind will not remain idle! If you fail to plant **desires** [bold added for emphasis] in your subconscious mind, it will feed upon the thoughts which reach it as the result of your neglect. (Hill, 2007)

Thoughts created by your mind are generally related to the events that you have experienced, the books you have read, the movies you have watched, or the music you have listened to. Your mind plays with different scenarios using only the images stored during these events.

The thoughts that You bring from the invisible world and plant in the garden of your mind are usually inexplicable to the mind: they're creative, joyful, and inspirational. I'm sure you have had these kinds of thoughts yourself, but you disregarded them or discredited them because they had no "logic" – they had no logic for your mind, would be the right way of saying it.

I remember a few instances when I had these kinds of thoughts, and at that time I couldn't explain them with my mind. On one occasion, I was home during the summer vacation from high school, which happened to be a boarding school. I woke up from a dream in which I saw myself in the new school year in a different classroom. More so, in particular, I was at the back of the class, while up until that time I never sat in the last row of a classroom, and I was leaning on a chair observing a conversation between a classmate and the teacher. The image was so vivid in my mind that I kept thinking of it all day struggling to make any sense of it, asking myself what it meant or what I was supposed to do with that information, because at that moment, at that time, it made no sense whatsoever.

The new school year began and here I was, back with my classmates, chatting and sharing memories of the summer break, when the teacher informed us that this year we would learn in a different classroom. The downside was that it had no benches, and we all had to go outside and carry our own as they were new and just delivered. As I wasn't particularly fond of following orders, or going with the herd, I skipped this activity and only showed up when all was settled.

As you can imagine, each carried his own bench and occupied the ones they carried. As I didn't carry any, I had to sit at the back of the class – on a chair.

The teacher showed up, and while sharing with us the details about the schedule for the year, found himself interrupted by one of my classmates chattering. The teacher asked my classmate to rise, and as I was leaning on my chair looking from the back at the event, I almost lost balance and was very close to falling down with the chair when the same image that I'd had in my mind that summer morning, a few weeks back, started rolling. It was like reliving the same event once again, like I was watching a clip that I've seen before; I could actually predict the words coming out of their mouths. The experience was mind-blowing. I was excited, shocked, and scared all at the same time.

I shared this experience with my classmates after the class, but as you can imagine, they were all trying to discredit my story because it couldn't be explained. It couldn't have been explained by a human mind, a limited-in-knowledge mind, and I didn't know that at the time.

On a different occasion I woke up to another inexplicable "dream." This time, I was at university, 600 km away from my girlfriend (my wife today), and the event that rolled in my mind showed me that I was a taxi driver in the city where my girlfriend was living and studying at university. So I called her and shared my dream. We both tried to make sense of it, and in the end we gave up on it as, again, we were trying to use our minds to explain something that the mind couldn't explain.

As soon as my last year at the university finished, I moved across the country to be closer to the love of my life.

Months went by looking for a job unsuccessfully. Eventually, I accepted an opportunity to drive a taxi for a lady who was looking for drivers, just to make some money to pay rent and eat until I found a "proper job." I can tell that you can see what's coming, and yes, one day as I was waiting in the taxi rank for my next fare, the film started rolling. This time, without hesitation, I took out my mobile and called my girlfriend. "Do you remember that day when I called and told you that I dreamt myself a taxi driver here?" This time I had someone to share my experience with, and I didn't feel like a lunatic. This time I didn't have doubts whether this actually happened or not. This time I knew that something the mind couldn't explain was happening and we are bigger than our minds.

Most of the time we try to explain certain events in our life through the limited ability of our mind, and we go on to read what others have to share in their discoveries and we try puzzling all the information together, but it still feels like an incomplete picture. Sometimes we simply give up, while other times we strive a little more in the pursuit of finding a suitable answer before we give up. Only those, who we now call the great spiritual leaders, who abandoned the idea of trying to comprehend with their mind the things that don't belong to the physical world, and surrendered to their real being, managed to understand the real meaning of their existence.

> **You have absolute control** [bold added for emphasis] over but one thing, and that is your thoughts. This is the most significant and inspiring of all facts known to us! It reflects our Divine nature. This Divine prerogative is the sole means by which you may control your own destiny. If you fail to control your own mind, you may be sure you will control nothing else. (Hill, 2007)

We have the capacity to observe the information that our mind holds in memory, and we have the power to choose to accept this information as true or false. The fact is, the information that we observe is neither true nor false; it's just information. It's us who make it true or not. It's us who give it life, ignore it, or discredit it.

When the mind labels an event as good or bad, it does that by using a reference point, a perspective, decided by the mind based on particular information. From one perspective a fish is a limbless cold-blooded vertebrate animal with gills and fins living wholly in water, from another standpoint a fish is life, and then from another perception a fish is food. All statements are true; it's only the mind and the principle to which the mind adheres that make these statements different.

There are people who eat animals, and there are people who love the animals and believe it's cruel to eat them. There are people who only love certain animals and eat other kinds of animals, as from their perspective some are cute or intelligent, while others serve as food. There are people who love meat but can't stand the idea of killing an animal. The only difference is in their view and their belief. There is no wrong or right; it's only a perception of the mind as wrong or right.

Whatever you believe to be true is true for you. Whenever you hear people judging other people for their beliefs, remember it's their mind labeling. You have no reason to judge another You, because

You and the other You are alike and judging the other You is judging You.

The mind compares, weighs, and measures, and does all these things to grasp a perception of its reality, and You can use these abilities to navigate through the physical world. However, when You see another You inhabiting a body in a different color, with a different voice, shape, or from a different continent, don't judge the model; admire You for the choice made and appreciate that You two have different journeys.

When the mind chooses to use the alleged information on other humans, it usually leads to comparisons, measurements, discrimination, hatred, jealousy, greed, and even to diseases and wars. When two people's minds measure themselves on intelligence, one may be superior because they read more and use their thinking more, while if measured on physical skills, the other might be superior because they spend the same amount of time on physical labor. Each one has different abilities due to the amount of time spent on specific activities.

You, the being in your body, doesn't need physical senses to perceive another You, because You are both the same, and when the You has a say in another You, it leads only to admiration and love. You see how much they've grown and evolved in their body and You are happy for their achievements, You appreciate them and congratulate them, and You share your love with them and that leads to harmony, wellbeing, wealth, and abundance.

We can tell the difference between those led by their mind from those who manage to control their mind through the level of judgement and comparison in their words and actions. When the mind is less evolved, like in children, you can observe them playing with other children and getting along very well regardless of race, social status, money, religion, country of origin, etc. The You being has full control in the actions and decisions of the body. Once the parent or tutor of the child, whose life is led by their mind, passes on information about the origin, color of skin, or abilities of the other children, that's when the little mind starts recording the differences and categorizes them.

If you find yourself in a judging or comparing situation with another person, remember that it's your mind talking, so pause, take a deep breath, and picture them as being You, then start over and see if you're still going to have the same level of judgment and comparison.

The happiest and most prosperous families are those in which the two partners respect, appreciate, and allow each other to manifest in their You element. When the relationship is based on looks or bank accounts, you can be sure that the partnership will only last as long as these perceptions exist, because they're based on the mind's measurements. There will always be someone who looks better, or someone with a bigger bank account. Then jealousy starts kicking in, then possessiveness, then arguments, then fights, and finally the dissipation of the relationship. If that ended there, it'd probably be just fine, but it goes further on throughout life to lead to regret and hatred, thoughts which only lead to disaster. The only people who ever managed to get over a broken relationship are those who forgave – didn't forget but forgave. Those ones who accepted that both their partner and themselves acted from a superficial judgement of the mind, and decided to forgive their actions so they wouldn't have to keep on judging whether they did or didn't do the right thing at the time, and also forgave their ex-partner for the same thing – those are the ones who moved on and managed to be happy later on. Others, as you may know, resume to intoxicating their mind and body with food, alcohol, drugs, or simply self-harming thoughts. Isn't it strange that they choose to harm themselves in retaliation?

Deep down, we know we're all the same and we understand that the actions that lead to fights and arguments come from the limited knowledge and ability of the mind, and quite often we allow our ego to take over and control the outcome, though if we manage to understand that we are not that ego, we are not that mind, and allow the real You to overflow its unlimited love, we'd forgive and accept whatever situation as part of the journey and move on.

Bob Proctor (2015) said, "The subconscious mind cannot tell the difference between what's real and what's imagined." The mind is simply a program that helps You control the body and the physical world You live in. Whatever You feed your mind will imprint in the physical world just as it is. "The mind is a superb instrument if used rightly," says Eckhart Tolle (2000), "used wrongly, however, it becomes very destructive."

Imagine, for instance, you're using a computer, and you want to print a photo. You can pick one from those saved in the memory of your computer, or you can create or upload a new image yourself. Whether you're using images already stored in the memory of your computer, which you can modify as you please, or you decide to create one from scratch, when you press print, that's the image that you'll have on paper. Whatever that image represents: love or hate, beauty or ugliness, peace or war, health or disease, it makes no difference to the computer. Your mind is just like that. Whatever images you bring up on its screen, whether you observe, modify, or create brand new ones, your mind will print them into the physical world regardless. Your mind manifests all of your thoughts and these can be either Yours or your mind's.

The mind works on its own, unless directed by You in a different direction. The earth will sprout all the seeds spread by the wind, regardless of their nature or origin – that's your mind for you. Cared for by a farmer, the earth will grow food; cared for by a florist, flowers will grow; abandon it and weeds will take over, and it's not because there are too many bad seeds in the world, but because there are too few people to look after their gardens.

> Mind control is the result of self-discipline and habit. You either control your mind or it controls you. There is no half-way compromise. (Hill, 2007)

If all people on this planet were to look after their thoughts and chose to share love and create beauty, there wouldn't be much bad seed left to be blown away by wind. There'd be only good seeds. Most of us have abandoned control of our minds and left things unattended. The media spreads out all sorts of seeds that create all the events that we observe in the world.

A medication commercial puts images of sickness and disease in every human mind watching it, both in the cared for minds and those that are not. The mind attended by You is cleaned, and these thoughts get removed before they have the chance to grow into sickness and disease, but an unattended mind will permit these seeds to take over, and these plants grow big and make seeds of their own and get blown by the wind and soon the whole world is taken over by them.

If you're thinking that this means we created the pandemics – you're right. We did create them, though not voluntarily. We created pandemics by not attending our own garden, our own mind, and allowed these seeds to grow and spread. And no, the pharma companies who created those commercials aren't responsible either. They may be one of the causes, indeed, but they haven't necessarily done it with the aim of spreading disease. There are multiple factors involved, and no, I don't defend them. I merely point out a source of the spread, not for your mind to judge them, but to make You aware that there are unwanted seeds spread over your garden so You can attend to it.

We also created financial recessions and depressions; we created climate change and we created tornadoes and tsunamis. We are all in this. Wake up and attend to your garden. Take care of your thoughts and you can bring change into the world – the kind of change that you want to see. Instead of watching news about wars, pandemics, financial crises, or natural disasters, change to something beautiful that you'd want to see. Watch a program that presents the beauty of the planet, or movies that picture happy and healthy families. Do you want to fix a pandemic? Stop fighting it! Stop feeding images of pandemics into your mind; simply plant images of health instead that will eventually outgrow the bad ones. Do you want to fix a financial crisis, or natural disasters? Stop feeding your mind with those kinds of images! Replace what you don't want with what you do want. Do you want to stop a war? Plant seeds of peace in your mind – see in your imagination the peace and harmony you want manifested, talk about peace, become peace!

Your mind may be kicking and judging right now, but only because that's how it's been programmed.

The media will tend to show images that, statistically, bring high ratings, because that's where the money is coming from. If we change the kind of programs we're watching, the media will start showing more of the programs that we're watching, which brings them higher ratings. Your mind may say it's cruel not to feel for the people who have been involved in those accidents and disasters shown, but watching the news or programs won't change what just happened. However, doing so will surely spread more of those images into the world, and worst of all, in your own garden. So unless you can physically go and help out those people in need, you don't need to watch that.

You have total control over your mind. No matter how messy your garden looks right now, you can change that! You can start bit by bit and replace the weeds with the seeds you want to grow in your garden, and soon your garden will be just the way You want it to be. Looking over the fence into your neighbor's garden won't fix yours, and if people passing by through your life admire your garden and the plants in it, they may even ask for some seeds for themselves.

Be an example of what you want the world to look like, but not by spreading seeds into your neighbor's garden – let them grow their own, and You look after yours. We are all in this together, and only by each of us doing our own part can we change the world. You may not be able to impress your neighbors to the extent that they will redesign their garden, but their kids may love what you've done with yours, and when they grow up, they'll remember. And if you teach your kids to plant good thoughts into their minds, your legacy will be carried on.

Shaping the mind

One way to make your mind work as you wish is by feeding its senses by using hearing, smell, touch, sight, and taste. This is the fastest way to reach the mind. Choose what you listen to, what you see, and associate good times with smells and tastes.

For instance, children born or adopted into riches, absorb the information fed to them through their senses: choice of foods, clean water, particular smells, and good quality clothing; they took that information and that became the norm in their mind. They keep those images in their mind and reproduce them over and over for the rest of their lives.

Children born in poverty absorb the information fed to them through the same senses: lack of food choice (or even lack of food), maybe dirty water, particular smells, poor quality clothing; they took that information and that became their norm – the norm in their mind. They also keep those images in their mind and reproduce them over and over for the rest of their lives – unless You change them.

When the two types meet, their minds are looking for reasons why the others are different, and because there is no relevant information stored in their minds, they ask their parents or tutors for clarification. Every adult had the chance in their longer life to look after their garden or not; some never learned they can pick specific seeds to plant, and based on their experience and attachment to their garden, they will justify the differences with words like "Rich people are bad" and "Poor people are lazy." Neither of these statements are true, and both the rich and the poor can confirm that. The rich give to charities to help noble causes, and the poor work very hard for the little they have.

But the seed that was fed into a child's mind starts growing into a big plant by the time they reach adulthood; the poor grow to detest the rich because they're bad, and the rich grow to detest the poor for not working hard enough. Can you see where I'm going with this? How many times have you encountered rich people showing no respect for the poor, or poor people judging and stealing from the rich?

These people aren't who they are because of what they are or where they were born but because of the information that was given to them and what their minds did with that information. You can take a poor child and put them in a rich family and the information that they receive will change the course of their "destiny" and vice-versa.

Even so, when they start growing up, and grow a mind of their own, they can change the course of their life by choice – by thinking themselves into their desires. A poor child may despise poverty so badly that their focus is only on getting rich, and they will end up doing anything to achieve their dream. A rich child may feel ignored by parents who are working all day every day to "maintain" that lifestyle and may choose to despise and separate from riches to find the love they thought they never had – and there are plenty of examples in the real world that you can observe for yourself.

The mind is the printer for your pictures and the earth for your seeds. What you feed into the printer or you plant into the ground can be 100% your choice. You decide whether to attend your garden or not, and what seeds you're going to plant. Feed your senses with all the images you want to see, all the sounds you love to hear, and all the smells and tastes you want to enjoy, and your mind will create more of them.

Most people make the mistake of not trying because they can't afford things, like not going to test drive a car they love or see a house they want, saying, "What's the point? I can't afford it anyway." But by not trying something, there is no information to feed to your mind. You need the picture of what you want your mind to create; you need that seed to plant in your garden.

Go and test drive that car you dream about: touch it, feel the smoothness of the finish, the smell of new, the way it accelerates, and how it makes you feel while driving it. Take those pictures in your memory and think about them to speed up the manifestation process.

Go and see that house you want to buy, walk in every room as if it's already yours, feel like home in it, and take the smell and all the details in your mind and design it yourself. Put your own furniture in it, paint the walls in the colors you want, and do all you want to do in that house in your mind as if you already own it. Nobody can take that away from you. Your thoughts are your own and what you do with them reflects into the life you live.

When you do this, when you see yourself already living that lifestyle, you've commanded the universe to deliver those thoughts and pictures, and opportunities will pop up from everywhere. People will say random things to you, or you'll hear random conversations that will trigger certain thoughts in your mind for you to act on them.

You'll see ads on TV or on billboards that will connect the dots from where you are to where you want to go, and an idea of a plan to achieve that goal will take form in your mind.

Salespeople understand this concept and they encourage their customers to test drive the cars or visit the houses; at the marketplace, salespeople provide samples of their goods for you to taste, clothing stores provide changing rooms so you can see how clothes look on you, perfume stores offer testers for you to smell, and makeup companies will even offer a makeup artist who can show on your own body how their products feel and look, and they'll do all they can to stimulate your senses and encourage you to buy.

Another amazing tool to shape your mind is autosuggestion. A statement repeated over and over will, eventually, overwrite beliefs impregnated in your mind by the environment to which it has been exposed. You want to train your mind to think the way you want: a house on the beach, a beautiful car, a happy family, and a healthy body, but the programming of your mind, the beliefs that have been impregnated, keep overriding these images and hold you back from achieving them, and before you know it, your mind wins.

Redefine your beliefs, reprogram your mind, and train it to work for you, not against you. Feed it new statements that help you manifest what you want. Your mind is your tool for You to use as You please. Take whatever belief your mind has that doesn't help you and override it with an affirmation. Show your mind that You are in charge and You are the one who controls it. Make "I am" statements for your mind so it can understand what You are: **I am health, I am wealth, I am love, I am prosperity, I am abundance, I am joy, I am intelligence, I am power, I am unlimited, I am strength, I am whole, I am perfect, and I am harmony.**

Saying these out loud stimulates the hearing, writing them stimulates the tactile sense, saying them in front of a mirror stimulates the sight, and together they stimulate a faster change in the belief system of your mind. Don't think You are feeding lies to your mind or allow your mind to make You feel ashamed of the statements. Your mind simply has been programmed one way, which most probably you had no control over, and it isn't the way You want it to be anymore because it manifests things and events that you don't want. Others have implanted beliefs in your mind and now it's time for You to plant your new truth in it:

I am health because I am the life pumping into my body. I am wealth because I am the creator of my own world. I am love because that is the nature of my being. I am prosperity because I can generate as many creative thoughts as I want. I am joy because I can experience this amazing world. I am intelligence because I am in direct contact with the universal consciousness. I am power because I am the source of my life. I am unlimited because I can reach anywhere with my thoughts. I am strength because I can do anything. I am whole because I am perfect. I am harmony because I can tune in to any feeling.

Say these out loud; feel the You expand from within, feel your heart pumping, and feel energy filling every cell of your body – that is the real You. So you see, You aren't lying; You're merely stating who You really are. Remind your mind who You are and that You are in charge.

> In all creation, in all eternity, in all the realms of your infinite being, the most wonderful fact is that You are God. You are the 'I AM that I AM'. You are consciousness. You are the creator. This is the mystery, this is the greatest secret known by the seers, prophets, and mystics throughout the ages. This is the truth that you can never know intellectually. Who is this you? That it is you, John Jones or Mary Smith, is absurd. It is the consciousness that knows you are

John Jones or Mary Smith. It is your greater self, your deeper self, your infinite being. Call it what you will. The important thing is that it is within you, it is you, it is your world. It is this fact that underlines the immutable law of assumption. It is upon this fact that your very existence is built. No, you cannot know this intellectually, you cannot debate it, you cannot substantiate it. You can only feel it. You can only be aware of it. (Goddard, 2019)

You are selfless and loving, You cares for others, and You loves everything that has life in it – because You are life. Your mind knows nothing of the sort. It has no feelings, only attachments. It doesn't create; it reacts. The mind pumps adrenaline into the body and pushes it into the "fight or flight" mechanism. Fear isn't within You, or in your body. Fear is in your mind. You are a timeless being bound to joy, love, and harmony.

You may control your own mind; you have the power to feed it whatever thought impulses you choose. With this privilege goes also the responsibility of using it constructively. You are the master of your own earthly destiny just as surely as you have the power to control your own thoughts. You may influence, direct, and eventually control your own environment, making your life what you want it to be, or you may neglect to exercise the privilege, which is yours, to make your life to order;

thus, casting yourself upon the broad sea of "circumstance" where you will be tossed hither and yon, like a chip on the waves of the ocean. (Hill, 2007)

Chapter 3

PURPOSE

The purpose of your body is to create and help You experience the creation. The telescope is useless without a human looking through it. The same as the body and mind is useless without You. You give purpose to your body by making the most of it.

It may seem like a mass of matter to the naked eye, but science has proven already that our body is a mass of energy vibrating on a specific level. As mentioned in the first chapter, our body is the gate between the two worlds – spiritual and physical. The spirit manifests into the physical world through our body, and through the body You experience the physical world.

As it's all energy, the only way for You to experience the warm touch of the sun; the smell of nature; the beauty of the night sky; the taste of foods; the sound of water falling, fire burning, birds tweeting, and so on, is through this beautiful body that You inhabit.

The body has the ability to change energy into matter. Every idea, every thought that you impregnate in the mind of your body, manifests one way or another into the physical world. The universe doesn't make the distinction between what our mind labels as good or bad; its purpose is simply to execute our thoughts, whatever they may be, by law. Similar to gravity – if you drop something, it falls; if you think, it manifests.

I hear a lot of people say, "You can do anything if you put your mind to it." In reality, it's not a matter of if – You **do** create anything your mind conceives, regardless of whether you want it or not. The only choice You have is in **what** it is being created. You can choose to create something that pleases You, or you can allow your mind to pick thoughts from your environment and let those thoughts be created. There are billions of people who are living a life dictated by their environment, their society, or their religion because they "think" they don't really have a choice, which leads me to the story of the baby elephant, that I heard in Jack Canfield's book The Success Principles.

The baby elephant is tied to a pole with a rope. As it's small, it doesn't have much power to break the rope, so it only moves as far as the rope allows it. As it grows up, even though its strength grows with it, its mind has learned that it can only go as far as the rope's length – its limitation is set by its mind, not its ability. The adult elephant is capable of pulling up to nine tonnes, but it's still limited by the length of the same rope it was tied with when it was just a baby. Only fire can scare the elephant enough to forget its limitation and break free, otherwise it would die of starvation and thirst before it breaks that rope.

That's how billions of people are living their lives. They're conditioned by the limitations of their society and have no clue they can go further. They feel tied to a pole, and limited by their belief in the length of the rope that keeps them grounded. Only when they go through a shocking event can they break the rope and discover they aren't confined by that limitation and can wander free.

I've come to realize that in an astonishing percentage of over ninety percent, people all over the world believe that the only way to make money is by working for a company, or someone else, and getting a salary – their belief is their reality; their limitation.

Some people believe that the only way to be happy in a relationship is to be "lucky" to find "the one" – as if there is only one person in the whole world who can make you happy and your job is to keep on searching through billions of people. Some choose to go with whomever they meet because they don't want to "risk" wasting their life in the search of the one; and that's why people become unhappy in marriages, and why separations are so high. Their belief is their limitation.

Some people believe that if they get sick, only a good doctor may be able to heal them. Doctors are then forced to filter through the amount of patients and raise their prices because of the high demand, and soon the people give up on their own life and hope for healing because they can't "afford" it financially. Their belief is their reality.

Whatever You think, or your mind believes, manifests into the physical world. Though, when we allow our mind to lead the way and we rely on the physical senses to tell us how to perceive the world, we say that "seeing is believing" – if you can see something with your own eyes, then you can believe it. That's not really believing – that's identification. Believing implies imagining a certain outcome that you know will happen and to expect it to happen; and by that belief you then are able to see its manifestation. **Believing is seeing**, not the other way around.

Do you believe you can walk? Don't look back into the past to remember whether you've done it before. Look into the present and see if you can do it right now. Look into the future and see yourself doing it. Yes, you can walk, and not because you've done it in the past but because your brain has been wired by your belief to make it so. Are you missing a leg, or both? Don't let circumstances determine your belief. Don't let circumstances wire your brain to hold you back from doing it. Close your eyes and see yourself walking, believe yourself to be walking, and you may not be able to grow limbs … yet, but surely a way will be shown for your belief to manifest, and if that belief is to walk, you will.

Do you believe you can earn more money? Answer honestly! Don't wish for it, and don't allow your current circumstances to limit your earning potential. Believe that you can! Believe that a way will be found to match the vision that you create on the screen of your mind. See yourself earning and spending that money and believe it to be true.

Do you believe you can find happiness? Are you happy now? Whatever your belief is, it matches your reality. So if you want to change your reality, change your belief, change your thoughts, and create the reality you want on the screen of your mind.

Look around you: kids are going to school; teens are getting diplomas and looking for jobs, fighting and competing against each other for a career; the elderly are retiring from work, living their last years happily or not, and everybody says this is the norm. If you observe the environment and believe it to be the norm, you create a "similar" norm for yourself.

Before I learned that we have the ability to create our own environment, I kept moving from one place to another in the hope of finding the "happy one." I moved from town to town in Romania and, in the end, to the United Kingdom in the search for this perfect environment. Years later, surrounded by a community of fellow migrants, I realized that we all changed the environment, but not everyone had adapted to the new environment. By sticking to their old habits and paradigms they changed the new environment instead. So I thought, if by bringing old habits into a new environment you can change it, by bringing new habits into an old environment you can change that also.

Take any culture, or any other country, and some may amaze you, while others may shock you when it comes to their norm, but they live their lives believing that is what a normal life is and their belief manifests into their reality. Some cultures believe the cow is sacred, while others would treat it as a good meal. Some cultures believe the dog is man's best friend, while others believe it can serve as a good dish. If any of these statements make you cringe, remember that's your mind's perception of the physical world we live in; that's your mind's cultural belief and your cultural belief is different from another's.

Whatever culture you were born into, its rules and standards have been impregnated into your mind through your physical senses: sight, hearing, tastes, smells, and touch. Your mind takes whatever it perceives through these senses, believes them to be true, and creates an environment that matches that belief. But remember – You are not your mind.

If a newborn was removed from any culture and moved across the world, that child would bring nothing from the environment in which it was born to the new one. Its mind hadn't matured enough to absorb the old environment to recreate it, so once the new environment reached its senses, this new environment became the norm that is recreated by the mind.

Now, take a moment to pick one successful person, or ten; pick one great leader, or ten; or simply pick them all. What do they all have in common? – nonconforming to what our mind calls the norm. They all believed that life **can** be different. They all believed that they **could** do something different for themselves. Some of them were dropouts from schools, some had never been employed, and none of them followed the norm of their society. We call them eccentrics or nonconformists, and we judge them and criticize them, but deep down we all want what they have. We all want to live their unique lives, but most of us want that without changing a thing in our habits, in our thoughts, and in our beliefs. Some even try to copy those lives in an attempt to replicate it. We don't realize that the world in which these successful people live is a design of their own that they played on the screen of their own minds. We fool ourselves by saying that we live in the same city or neighborhood, we've been to the same school, we have the same diploma, and so on, and we expect the same outcome, but the difference isn't in the physical – it's in the mind of each and every one of us. We manifest the reality that we believe in our minds.

What's in your mind? What do you believe?

Some of those who succeeded came from broken families where there was no unity or constraints for them to stick to a particular norm; some changed environments; or ran away from their old environment into a "new land" where they broke free from their old habits, created a new version of themselves in their own mind, and changed their habits to match that. They achieved their success because they believed they could, and everything else changed because of their belief.

You have a choice. You can either observe and conform to what you see or believe in your own custom designed dream and make that happen. If you want change, You have to be the change. If you want the world to be different, You have to be different. If you want your children to live in a better world, You have to become a creator of an ideal world, and an example they can emulate. The power is within You.

If every individual who reads this book starts thinking and starts believing that they can live a life of their own design, they will. And when all these individuals start living the life of their own design, a shift in the norm begins to happen, and the rest of the world will then see a new norm that they will observe and believe to be true, and then they will live a new kind of norm. So by changing your beliefs, by changing your life, you actually are changing the whole world. You **are** the change. You **are** the world.

Whenever you ask yourself, "What's my purpose in this life?" remember that your purpose is to create, to change, to be the change, and to lead others to a happy and fulfilled life by living a happy and fulfilled life yourself, and you can do this by changing one thing – the nature of your limitation. Believe that you can have the life you want. Believe that You are a limitless being. Believe that you are not a product of your environment but a product of Your own thoughts.

> *"The opposite of courage in our society is not cowardice, it is conformity."*
>
> *—Rollo May*

You may choose to ignore this information, or you may choose to discredit it, so I'm going to tell you this: It's not You who does that; it's your mind. Your mind is incapable of believing without seeing, your mind is incapable of accepting something without proof, and I encourage You to look back in your life and recall the moments when all the odds were against you but for "some" reason You knew you could make it, or You knew you could get through or get away from. That deep feeling of "knowing," that's your belief; that's what determines the difference between You and your mind.

*"Whether you think you can, or
you think you can't, you're right."*

—*Henry Ford*

So I encourage you to discredit this information **only after** you've tested this theory. But keep in mind this, if you're looking for reasons to discredit this information, you will find them, and your mind will be the first to point them out. If you open your mind and look for reasons why it could work, or the benefits you may have if this proves right, you will find them. Whatever you're looking for, you will find it. How can I prove this? Very simply actually. Tonight, when you go to bed, close your eyes and think of all the bad luck you had today, think of all the people who hurt your feelings, all those who cut you off in traffic, and think of all the fights you've had and everything that went wrong. When you wake up tomorrow morning, think of all the reasons why your day will be the worst day of your life. Blame everything outside of you for whatever goes wrong. Start with the weather – look for all the reasons why the weather is bad, and even if it's sunny, just say you hate it because the sun makes you squint; blame the traffic, the people you meet, the job, and everything that comes your way. Think all the bad and negative thoughts that you can for one day, and at the end of the day, write down, in an objective way, your discovery. How did you feel? How did things turn out? How many good things happened to you, and how many bad things happened?

In the evening, do the exact opposite of the previous night. Close your eyes when you go to bed and think of all that you've been blessed with throughout your life – ignore the last day as you may not be able to find much there – and recall all the amazing things that happened to you all the way from your earliest childhood memories up until today; the roof above your head; the car, or cars; family; and the moments you felt great – be grateful for them with all your heart and drift off to sleep in the most amazing memories. When you wake up in the morning, think of all the reasons why this day will be the best day of your life, look for goodness in everything, and be grateful for everything that will happen this day with the thought that You created this amazing day with your amazing memories from the night before. And if anything bad happens (could be residual thoughts from the past), try to find the good in it (in every circumstance there are always two sides); if the weather is bad, just think of it as good for the nature; if anyone cuts you off in traffic, let them be – they might be in a hurry to get somewhere. If your boss shouts at you, just imagine they may have been shouted at by their boss. If your spouse or kids upset you, remind them that you love them very much. At the end of the day, in an objective way, look back on your day and write down your discovery. How did you feel? How did things turn out? How many good things happened to you, and how many bad things happened? Then compare the notes from the two days.

You won't be surprised to realize that both days turned out exactly as you **thought** they would. You won't be surprised because You **knew** that's how they would turn out to be. You **know** that's how things work; deep down You already **know** this truth that your mind has beclouded with "lack of proof – if you can't see it, it can't be true."

You are the creator of both these two days. Your thoughts created all the circumstances and events that you have encountered throughout the day, and your mind helped You by pointing them out, which only proves that your mind is your tool to use, and You are its master. You are the power that creates the day. You are the power that creates every day. Your thoughts give shape to every event in your life.

Chapter 4

THOUGHTS, EMOTIONS AND FEELINGS

Humans have been in the grip of pain for eons, ever since they fell from the state of grace, entered the realm of time and mind, and lost awareness of Being. At that point, they started to perceive themselves as meaningless fragments in an alien universe, unconnected to the Source and to each other.
(Tolle, 2000)

There is a universal language that each and every person on this earth is using, but not many understand it. This language isn't spoken and yet is heard, doesn't have words and yet has messages, and doesn't use grammar and yet it makes perfect sense. This is the language of your being; the same being that exists within each and every one of us –

You. The channel of communication for this language through our bodies is our feelings (as mentioned in the second chapter). We feel the happiness within us through our body and the happiness within others. We feel the joy and sadness in us, and in all the people with whom we connect. The closer two people are, the stronger the connection between them. It's often described as telepathy, premonition, clairvoyance, etc.

The more control You have over your body and mind, the easier it is to connect with others and to perceive their feelings. Very often we allow our mind to take control of our conversations and try to "read" the physical signals in others. Unlike conversing with the mind, being You doesn't require any effort at all to communicate. You only have to let go of any resistance that comes from the mind. Words were created by the mind – it's the language of the mind, not yours.

It's You who has the ability to communicate with other people, generally close to you, through the principle known as telepathy. You may have experienced situations when you were thinking of a person and they called you or wrote to you.

It's You who draws information from the universal consciousness when new ideas are born. Napoleon Hill (2007), in his book *Think and Grow Rich*, called it "Creative Imagination." The mind merely has the ability to work with the information stored in its memory, rearranging old concepts, ideas, or plans into new combinations; this is described by the same author as "Synthetic Imagination."

Emotions and feelings are the language of You. They're your way of communicating with other beings and with your own body. It's You talking to nature, people, animals, and especially your body, and You are also the one feeling them through your body.

Before the human language was created, people would communicate through their feelings. A newborn feels their mother's love; a mother feels her baby's distress. The leader of a tribe would have been the one who felt confident and powerful, and the rest of its members would follow the power they were feeling from the leader. In fights it was never the strength that won but the confidence, the fearlessness.

As the mind of humans evolved, sounds started coming out of their mouths, which formed messages when associated with particular actions, and through the evolution, languages have been created. The reason we only have less than 7,000 languages spoken today is because people have united throughout time, and many of the original languages were fused together, have been incorporated, or simply have disappeared due to lack of usage and speakers (Linguistic Society of America). Every mind, originally, created its own language that was shared with the family or tribe. Most children, when they discover their ability to articulate sounds, make up words that we call gibberish. Only after the parents insist on using specific words to define specific objects, things, and actions, does the child's mind conform to the family's language.

When the mind is incapable of transmitting a message through its programming, something bigger than the mind takes charge and that is You. You communicates through love, affection, care, patience, and generosity.

You listen with the "heart," not with the ears. Two children, while playing, will always have a good time together, regardless of the language they speak, or if they speak a language at all.

The language as you know it is a product of the mind. If a child is moved anywhere in the world, their mind will learn the spoken language of the locals. You, reading this book, may already know a couple of languages and you can still learn more, but when you travel anywhere in the world and meet people with whom you don't have a common language, you're still able to communicate. And you may think that you're using some rudimentary sign language, but when did you learn sign language? Isn't this a manifestation of You through your body? Isn't this something you **feel** that comes **naturally**?

There are studies showing that feelings are some sort of brain activity releasing specific chemicals into the body making you feel the emotions (Kandler, 2019). My argument is that's You manifesting through the body. You – the love and the life in the body – are the very cause of these chemical reactions. You are the one triggering that tingling feeling when you meet the love of your life, that comforting sensation in the arms of the one who you love, and energy that gives you power to move mountains whenever you want to.

The mind has also learned to stimulate the body in a similar way in order to protect it. The dominant feeling of the mind is fear – fear of harm from exterior elements to the body. Fear has the role to protect the body. It releases chemicals into the body and impulses you to seek shelter from the weather, to seek food and clothing, to run from danger or fight it. Though it may seem like all feelings have the same origin, they don't. They may feel the same way through the body, but their cause is different. The mind learned to emulate the manifestation of feelings by releasing chemicals into the body; therefore, creating a "similar" sensation.

The dominant feeling of You is love.
The dominant feeling of the mind is fear.

All the other feelings are derived from one of these two. Love is how You express your being, while fear is how the mind protects the body. Love is expanding, while fear is contracting.

The mind only exists as long as the brain exists. And the brain exists as long as there is a body to support, feed, and oxygenate the brain. So when the mind takes control of the body, all decisions and actions come from fear – from the need to protect the body. You don't jump off heights because your mind fears harming the body. You don't eat foods that you learned can harm your body and make it sick, and you may not even eat any foods that you don't know. However, when the life of a fellow human, and especially a close one, is at stake, the You takes charge, and You find yourself putting the life of your own body at risk out of love for the life of the ones in danger. You, the love and life, knows the body isn't its limitation; You knows there is no death beyond the body but more life in a different form.

There are countless examples of people becoming heroes for risking the life of their body to save others doing "impossible" things, like lifting cars, walking through fire, fighting beasts, and so on. The You in these people has taken full control of the actions of their body by shutting down the mind and inhibiting its fears, for the time being, to protect the life of another You – because You are love and life. Some of these people can't even believe they've actually been capable of doing that after the event.

You, love, and life are one and the same thing – the same manifestation into the body and through the body. You always seek to expand life and share love.

In the bodies mostly controlled by the mind, the predominating feeling is fear and all the feelings derived from fear. Napoleon Hill (2007) compiled a list of the main fears that control the actions of the mind. These are: the fear of death, fear of sickness, fear of old age, fear of loss of love from someone, fear of criticism, and fear of poverty. Out of these are born the feelings of jealousy, hate, revenge, greed, superstition, anger, etc. If any or more of these control your decisions and actions, just know that you are the prisoner of that or those fears, but You can break free if your desire is strong enough. No walls built by your mind can hold You, unless you allow it.

I lived near a monastery for five years while in boarding school. There were people bringing their loved ones to the monastery claiming that they were possessed and would put their faith in the holy men and their prayers to release the body of their loved one from the evil spirits. I never really understood as an adolescent what was really happening, as the idea of a good God allowing evil spirits sounded a bit far-fetched. Now, I know that those people were taken over by the fears of their minds to a degree that the You in them was like a prisoner in a forgotten cell at the bottom of a pit. Fear was, in essence, the actual evil possessing the body and driving the mind mad. The act of exorcism the priests were performing was more of a resuscitation of the You in the body – a call out.

Any action of the mind goes through the filter of one of these fears, while any action of You comes from love. Remember this next time you make a decision, or when you take any action.

Feelings play a very important role in the process of manifestation – they're the fuel of the process. Any kind of emotion applied to any kind of thought speeds up its manifestation.

When I was just a kid, and still using rotary corded phones, I imagined a phone that could be operated by a battery and I could carry around so my parents could reach me when they wanted me to come home.

My father used to work in a factory on an airfield, building military planes. One day he took me in to show me around and I got to ride an electric vehicle used to move parts around, and I started thinking, "How cool would it be if all the cars on the streets could be operated like that," as it seemed really complicated in my little mind the whole "changing gears" thing.

Both examples have been manifested; the universe responds to all our thoughts, whatever they are, but the speed of their manifestation into our life is determined by our feelings. If you want them, you have to feel as if you already have them. Today I don't leave my home without a mobile phone in my pocket, and I drive a car that plugs into a wall and runs on battery power. My thoughts as a child created the things I was imagining, and my emotional involvement with those ideas manifested them in my life.

Through thoughts and emotions, I manifested my perfect partner (at the time of writing this we've been happily together for over twenty-one years and I can't remember a time that I didn't love her), I manifested the life I'm living, the house, the model and color of my car, and this book – and I'm still manifesting every day of my life the way I want it with the power of my thoughts and feelings.

You, too, have manifested the life you live right now with your thoughts and emotions, whether it's one that you like or not. The manifestation process depends entirely on the thoughts you have and the feelings you apply to them. If, so far, you've been afraid to act on certain things you thought of, those thoughts still manifested into your life, regardless of your inaction, because you had the thought and the emotion – you were afraid of the possible results. If you acted on the thoughts you were afraid of, you only speeded up the process. Equally, the thoughts associated with love, or a "burning desire," manifested in the same manner, whether you acted on them and helped the process or you didn't and just allowed the universe to follow its course.

Everything exists in a state of vibration, or energy. If you take any object around you and put it under the microscope, you'll discover that energy is what gives form to matter. What we generally call matter is made up of atoms, in which only 0.0001% is the actual matter, while the rest of 99.9999% is the energy that holds the atom together (Dispenza, 2020). Matter as we know it can't exist without the energy that holds it together.

Energy is a state of vibration. The level of vibration determines the shape of the physical thing that we perceive with our senses. By adding heat (energy) to a glass of water, we're changing its level of vibration and it becomes what we perceive as steam; by taking heat (energy) away from the same glass of water, we're changing its level of vibration and it becomes what we perceive as ice.

Sound is also energy, which moves in different forms of vibration. If you get a closer look at the membrane of a speaker, you can see that it changes its vibration based on the sound it makes – high sounds relate to high vibration and low sounds to low vibration. Light is also energy, which moves on even higher forms of vibration than sound. Different vibrations determine – in our mind's perception – different colors. At a vibration of approx. 700 nanometers we perceive it as red and at approx. 400 nanometers, we perceive it as violet; the rest of the rainbow colors are in between. At vibrations higher than this spectrum is the light we call ultraviolet, only perceived by a handful of people, bees, dogs, and some other animals. At vibrations lower than this spectrum is infrared. Night-vision goggles work by detecting infrared light, also associated with heat. At an even higher vibration we have the energy that we call Gamma ray and X-ray. At the opposite end we go to microwaves and radio waves (the Physics Classroom).

I hope this helps you understand that by changing the vibration of the energy we perceive through our physical senses, the matter itself is changing. The energy is the same; its vibration, however, changes the physical property, the manifestation, of the physical object. Chemistry is, in essence, the art of changing the vibration of energy.

Thought is energy at the highest state of vibration. The same as radio waves, sound, and light traveling through matter, time, and space, thoughts also travel through matter, time, and space. The same way you tune a radio to a specific frequency to receive the broadcast from a specific station, in order to perceive particular thoughts, you have to tune to their frequency, to their level of vibration, to experience and manifest them.

We've seen how by changing the level of vibration of ice, it becomes liquid and then steam, sound becomes ultrasound, and radio waves become microwaves. Thoughts also change their level of vibration by mixing them with the energy of emotion. Picture yourself as the broadcasting station of your own thoughts. All you think is broadcasted on a specific frequency – one that is unique to you. This frequency is determined by your paradigm, which is the total sum of your beliefs.

The receiver of your thoughts is the universe at large, which takes the form and shape of your messages by mixing your 99.9999% thought energy with the 0.0001% matter that exists in the universe to bring into physical form what is broadcasted by your paradigm.

The moment you understand that your thoughts determine the life you live, you'll start watching your thoughts, you'll pick those that you want to manifest in your life, and you'll fill them with feelings of love and gratitude, which makes the process of manifestation even faster. When you have thoughts of things that you don't want in your life, simply ignore them and let them slide; as long as you don't involve yourself emotionally with them, you can rest assured that they will take a while before they manifest – if they ever manifest. Yes, if they ever manifest. I know it sounds a bit confusing after stating that all thoughts manifest, so allow me to explain.

When you have a thought, the universe starts working and rearranging itself toward the manifestation of that thought as that's your command. In the meantime, another thing happens: your mind observes the thought, thinks the thought over, and over again, and again, and multiplies that thought; therefore, sending even more commands to the universe – like a cascade of thoughts. So when you think of something that you don't want, a message is sent into the universe and the mind produces similar thoughts, which start sending similar messages – that is bound to happen. But if you catch that thought and replace it with a positive thought of something that you want to happen instead, even though the command for the original thought was sent into the universe for its manifestation, you stop the cascade of negative thoughts and replace it with a cascade of positive ones. So if the predominating thoughts that follow in your mind don't harmonize with the original thought, it will make the manifestation of the original thought become significantly small and barely detectable.

I know someone who wanted to scam a car insurance company by causing an accident. He was planning to suddenly stop the car so the one behind wouldn't have time to react and would bump into his rear, so he played that thought in his mind over and over. I asked him to think of the people in the car behind who may suffer – who knows what kind of injuries he would be directly responsible for. He agreed that it was probably not the best option and scrapped his plan. However, he didn't replace his thoughts with something that he wanted instead, so a few weeks later, the universe delivered on its promise. As he was driving, he legitimately stopped to give way in traffic. The driver behind wasn't paying attention and rammed into his rear, manifesting the exact scenario he had in his mind when he was planning to scam the insurance company.

If, at that time, I had known the power that our thoughts have, I would've advised him to shift his daily thoughts in the opposite direction, and create a different scenario to play in his mind in which the driver behind would stop in time and everybody happily carried on with their own life. I would've told him that the power that we have, to manifest into the physical plane the thoughts that we create in our mind, works whether we want it to or not. And I would've told him that the law of attraction acts in the same manner as the law of gravity or any other physical law works – precisely and impersonally.

So if after you've seen an accident and you thought of the accident, even though you started moving the universe in that direction, you can change your thoughts in a positive direction and adopt a positive attitude, like "I'm protected," "Thank God that's not me," "I'm so grateful that I wasn't going that way," or any other kind of thoughts that counterbalance the thought of an accident. The manifestation of your original thought may turn out to be just a toe bump or a papercut – still an accident but not of the same proportions. Your predominant thoughts determine the direction of your life.

If you wonder why not all of your good thoughts manifest, the reason is in the same principle. You may think that you want to be successful, and you imagine yourself as that, and in the process, you've commanded the universe to deliver to you a successful life. The universe, in that instant, starts working toward rearranging itself to deliver your request. But if, after you've finished that thought, day-dream, visualization process, or whatever it was that you intentionally created, you go back to your routine thoughts that you create based on the observations around you, like "Oh, no, another bill. I can't afford this," or "My boss didn't see my achievement – again. He never does," or "All the online businesses are scams," or "My business is like a small fish in an ocean of sharks," the universe turns toward the new commands and starts working on delivering those instead, and your original desire may only manifest as a discount in a superstore, a pat on the back, or a smile. You may have made a small step toward your dream, but after that you've made even more steps in the opposite direction.

In other words, the more positive thoughts you put in your mind, the better your life will be. Now, in order to create a life by design, you'll have to pick the thoughts that you want manifesting in your life and dwell on them for as long as it takes to manifest, keeping in mind, though, your previous thoughts may have moved the universe in a different direction, and it may take a bit longer for the new ones to manifest, but if you keep at it and fill your mind all day every day with the thoughts of your desire, you can't fail in achieving it.

The only battle you have to fight is with your own mind, which lives in a little fortress. If you keep hitting it with positive thoughts over and over, its walls will eventually crumble. Don't give up until the walls are down. Once you've conquered your mind, you've conquered life.

When using your emotions, you're fueling the power of the universe, and you're no longer waiting for the right circumstances to arrange themselves to have what you want. When applying the power of your emotions, you speed up the manifestation of the thoughts that roam your mind. The better you know how to control your emotions, the easier it is to use them in your favor.

Emotions, both love based and fear based, are equally powerful because they engage the body, which is the medium for manifestation – how your body vibrates resonates with the life you live. When we are born, love flows through our body like the blood flows through our veins; that's why people are enthralled by newborn babies – they feel that powerful feeling of love and they allow themselves to be drawn toward it. As the mind starts evolving, a new feeling comes along – fear. Our thoughts are equally influenced by the force of these emotions. A strong emotion of love for someone will push your body to do things you wouldn't do otherwise, and the only thing that can stop you from doing them is your own mind, which only aims to protect your body.

When you deliberately apply feelings or emotions to your thoughts, the power of You is employed to drive and motivate your body; You become the moving force of the world around you and draw from the universe all that is required for fast, or instant, manifestation of the thought charged with emotion. What we call desire is a thought – an idea emotionalized. The stronger the emotion, the stronger the desire is.

When people like Edison, the Wright brothers, Tesla, Jobs, Bezos, and Musk were taken over by their desires, they were driven by a force bigger than their physical body, and they were energized to work tirelessly until the fulfilment of that desire.

You may not always have much action to take, or your mind may not have the necessary knowledge to act in that direction, or maybe sometimes there is nothing you can physically do to get closer to the manifestation of your desire, but if you keep fueling your thought or idea, and if you keep emotionalizing that desire so it becomes what Napoleon Hill (2007) calls "a burning desire," the force of the universe will come even stronger to support you.

For your thought, the universe opens all of its channels of communication to reach all the right people; it drives them to act, through an impulse they can't explain, and come to the aid of your burning desire. You can say that people are the instruments of our own desires in the same way we are the instruments of other people's desires. There are people who want to run a successful business and people who are looking for jobs – when the two types meet, each of them serves as an instrument for the other's desire. The only difference between the two is within their own desire.

When my wife and I went to buy our first home, we didn't have the necessary money to do that, but we wanted it really badly, so we went ahead, paid the reservation fee, and started all the procedures for the purchase of the house as if we already had all the money we needed. And I remember, every evening I'd drive to the new house, which wasn't even finished yet, park in the allocated parking space, turn off the engine, close my eyes, and imagine getting out of the vehicle, walking to the door, unlocking it, getting in, and shouting, "Honey, I'm hooooome!" Then I would think of different scenarios of what we'd do in our new home, and I felt that emotion of walking into my own home, the smell of the new house, and that feeling of satisfaction that I got the house. I still shout, "Honey, I'm hooooome!" when I come back after a long day, though this time around I do it out loud, but it's still the same house I used to park outside of and visualize myself in it.

A force bigger than us was working on our behalf because people were coming out of the blue to support and help us with ideas and with the whole process, while our biggest concerns remained to be the kind of furniture and color of paint to have in each room.

I did the same thing with the car. I wanted a specific electric model and color. I went for a test drive and absorbed every single detail of it into my mind. After the test drive, I got back into my old car and imagined I was driving the brand new one that I had just tested, with all the details that I could recall and how the wheel and seats felt, pretending I couldn't hear the engine, though it was a noisy diesel.

One particular thing I visualized was how people would turn their heads around admiring my new car. That visualization became my reality. After I had the new car delivered and I was driving it around, people were literally turning their heads.

For months I had these "flashbacks" – they were in fact the manifestation of the thoughts I created and emotionalized in my mind.

The manifestation process isn't a matter of if but a matter of when, and that relates directly to the level of emotion that you apply to the thoughts you want to manifest. The stronger the feelings you apply to your thoughts, the faster you get to really live those thoughts in the physical plane.

Most people aren't aware of this law of the universe through which You manifests the thoughts of your mind into the physical world through the vibration of your body. They allow their mind to create fear-based thoughts instead, dwell on them, and even become emotionally involved with them. They allow their mind to create scenarios involving fear: the fear of losing someone, fear of not being able to get a particular job, fear of being criticized or being laughed at, or fear of not being able to meet parents' expectations, and whatever they're afraid of, or have negative thoughts about, then leads to the manifestation of those thoughts charged with the emotion of fear.

I learned this from experience as I also allowed my mind to control my life with fear, and whatever I tried ended up in failure. Every venture and business opportunity turned out to be just another dead end and waste of time and money. I was so overwhelmed by fear that it started growing inside me and brought its friends along: fear of criticism, fear of poverty, fear of being stuck, and fear of losing what I had left.

Thoughts attract similar thoughts, and the more you have of a kind, the more of the same kind you get. One day I thought, if I was able to manifest all these things that I wanted with my mind, with the same mind I could also lose them if I lived in fear of losing them. That's when I realized the importance of gratitude in shaping one's mind.

So from thenceforth, whenever I had a fear-based thought, I'd turn toward the things I was grateful for and fill my mind with them. If I had a fear of losing my loved one, which usually leads to jealousy, I'd think of all the great times we'd had together and be grateful; if thoughts of not having enough money flooded my mind, I'd think of all the times I had money and be grateful for it; thoughts of sickness – I'd be grateful for the health that still was in my body, and so on.

Also, I'd create scenarios in my mind thinking that whatever hardship I was going through was happening for a greater good, like making new friends, discovering new places or things, or whatever I could imagine as a positive outcome. I'd accept whatever it was as part of a bigger journey, as a necessity for the discovery of clues or signs. I kept on feeding my mind positive thoughts and positive outcomes, and my life started changing and the universe started delivering a wonderful life filled with miracles at every corner.

It can be hard to be grateful when the car breaks down miles away from home when you have no money in your pocket and no roadside assistance because the policy ran out the day before and you wanted to wait until the next payday to renew it.

It can be hard to be grateful when your spouse/ partner no longer wants to be with you and leaves with your best friend. It can be really hard to be grateful in tough situations. But with a shift of thoughts and a change of focus you will find all the things to be grateful for in that moment. And maybe you'll have to call your father, mother, or old friend, with whom you haven't spoken in years, to come to help you out and reconnect with them. And maybe you'll meet someone who loves you for who you are and you end up much happier than before.

Miracles do happen when we are grateful. We can really move mountains, change hearts, bring people in around us, and move our life in the direction of our thoughts, and not by force – those who do that by force pay the price accordingly – but by thought alone with gratitude and love for the creation, because, in the end, your whole world is your own creation.

If you think about it, everything that exists, whether discovered by mistake by a "ordinary" person or laboriously designed by a genius, whether handmade by an underpaid human being in a forgotten corner of the world or precision built by a complex robot designed by another, is all part of the same world. We are all part of the same world, and we are cogs in the same massive existence on this planet, and there is no one more important that the other because one couldn't have the life they have without the other.

For you to sip your coffee or tea while reading this book to be possible, the labor of millions of people throughout time was necessary. From farmers and pickers, to storers and movers, to roasters and packers, designers, transporters, distributors, and storekeepers – you wouldn't have the coffee or tea in your house if it wasn't for them. To brew it involves another list of people. From the extraction of the ore and oil, and the production of metals and plastics required for the building of the kettle or the coffee maker. The mug you're using requires another set of people. And before you get to the book, don't forget what you're sitting on and how many people were required to build it, what you're wearing, where you're living, and so on.

We are all interconnected both physically and spiritually. We are all part of the same matter and the same energy that shapes this physical world. Feelings are the way through which we communicate – our language. When we suppress our love-derived emotions, we actually allow the mind to take control of the body and inhibit you. Then fear takes over the body.

The robot uprise, which we sometimes see in sci-fi movies, has already begun – only the robots in this instance aren't created out of titanium and steel but out of flesh and blood; our creation uprises against You because it "thinks" that You are too soft and mellow for this earth, while the existence of the human at the top of food chain must be associated with strength. The survival of the fittest is for animals, not for humans, but when we push the You out, all that remains is the animal with a highly evolved brain and a mind of its own.

When the mind controls the actions of the individual through its filter of fear, the main goal is to protect the individual at any cost – including that of another human's life; people controlled by their mind hurt and even kill each other just to protect themselves. The second goal is to rise above its peers through competitions and achievements – to get ahead of others. Though, most of the time the fear of criticism, and fear of failure, holds one back in the protective blanket of their comfort zone.

Some go to a job interview fearful that they may be judged by their peers if they, somehow, fail to get that job, or because they believe it to be their only option to get ahead in life. Once they get into the job, they realize it's not quite the job they wanted, but they're afraid to leave in case they land on an even more unsuitable job, thinking they had already gotten used to the worst of this job anyway and they can bear it a little bit longer. The more they dwell on the things they don't like about their current job, the worse it gets. Their negative thoughts bring about similar thoughts, but the mind adapts and carries on bearing the job until they get to the point they literally start hating it – just another way of creating emotions out of thoughts. And when they think this can't get any worse, they end up being laid off.

The one not fully chained by the mind who goes joyfully and confidently to a job interview, open to whatever life has to offer, has the highest chance of getting it. The interviewer, who usually goes through a series of questions, will feel this one has that *je ne sais quoi*, which attracts the interviewer, and they give them the job. Once in, they start showing gratitude for the opportunity and start working toward paying back for the opportunity.

The more they focus on doing more, the more appreciation they get, and the more appreciation they get, the more they happily and gratefully give back, and the circle carries on like this – pushing the individual into promotions and financial remuneration.

In the two examples, a shift in the thoughts and emotions brings a shift into the evolution of things. My last experience as employed started with thoughts of "What would I do if I were in charge." A position was offered to me and I did all that I thought I'd do; and while doing that I noticed other things that I could do if I had been in a different position and thought of them. Shortly after, that position became available and was offered to me. Because I already had in my mind what to do, I got right into them; then other thoughts started growing in my mind of the things I'd do if I were a manager and, as you can imagine, the position opened and was offered to me, and I did exactly what I had in mind to do.

At this point, after a very short period of time, something happened, and a shift of thoughts occurred in my mind. I was no longer grateful for the opportunity given, I allowed the circumstances to control me, and I felt abandoned somehow. Looking back, I could have used this as an opportunity to be promoted further, but instead I focused on the extra work that was expected of me and became dissatisfied with the pay, and the more I dwelled on these thoughts the worse it got, until one day I reached the bottom of the pit. I remember feeling sick just hearing the phone ring. The next day, I went in and quit. That's how, unconsciously, I shifted from a fast-ascending career to an abrupt ending.

In the moments of stress and despair, the mind looks for others to blame for the situations and circumstances, for it can't see its own errors. In truth, the mind did exactly as it was programmed to do; it did everything as requested, but being limited to its programming, it couldn't accept an error in its judgement. This is why, sometimes, you observe people "in the wrong" struggling to convince others they did the right thing, which from the limited perspective of their mind, they did. Even Hitler, from his mind's perspective, did all for good reasons – his mind's reasons. His desire of creating an "ideal state" went into action, though it disregarded the lives of others.

The mind doesn't have an equal perception of right or wrong in relation to other individuals because there is no real connection between two minds other than the laws of a state, a religion, or a tradition. What is right for some may be irrelevant or even wrong for others. There are cultures where eating pork and drinking alcohol are prohibited, while selling women as brides and treating them as possessions is a norm. There are places on Earth where not having a degree makes one feel like a reject of society, while in other places there are no schools.

Whatever these people observe, believe, and think becomes their reality, and one's dream life may be another's nightmare. From the moment of birth, the child's mind is fed, voluntarily or not, with the information of the environment, and the mind accepts whatever it receives through its senses as being **the truth**.

You, on the other hand, have a different perception of the truth, but this perception only manifests when You control the actions of the body. You can override the original programming for the purpose of manifesting your own truth. Whether you take this truth from another environment or you take it from the invisible world of love and life that you feel within, you can reprogram your mind to manifest whatever you want and believe to be the truth for You; therefore, creating Your Own Universe.

Your thoughts influence your feelings the same way your feelings influence your thoughts. In other words, You can decide to manifest love in your body, and joy starts inundating your mind causing it to manifest thoughts of love, happiness, and bliss, or You can allow the mind to observe the physical world and create its own thoughts, which will then trigger fear derived emotions associated with those thoughts, and causing it to manifest them instead.

The mind has been designed to help You, support You, and execute any order and thought that You give to it. The mind is nothing but a tool that helps You experience life on this earth. You are the master of the body and of your world. The mind is the executioner of your will, but if you let the executioner loose, it will do its own thing.

Observe your feelings as you go on with your day-to-day routine. Becoming an observer, you also become a participant in the course of your life. When you observe your feelings associated with the actions of your body, you'll know its outcome, even before you take that action.

Say, for instance, a friend asks you to go out one evening for a meal and drinks. If you don't feel good about it, you already know that, and thoughts start flooding your mind with possible scenarios of how that evening isn't going to be enjoyable or will turn out to be a disaster. However, when asked the same question, if a feeling of joy and excitement floods your body, You know it's going to be the best night ever and thoughts about how that's going to happen pop up in your mind. In both situations, your thoughts about that evening will manifest accordingly, but the feeling, the vibration, of your body not only gives you a preview of what's it's going to be like, it is also the catalyst that makes it your reality, and it's down to you and your choice whether that evening will carry on or not.

Yes, there are friends who can lift your spirits, and what you think and feel as being a wrong idea may turn out to be the exact opposite, but that is conditioned by your willingness to allow yourself to be guided by that person's feelings and emotions, though not all people have the same definition of fun.

Your feelings are messages that both You and your mind give to your body about a situation that is about to follow. If it's a feeling of excitement, joy, love, growth, or expansion, that is a signal from You. If the feeling is fear, it makes you anxious, holds you back, and you get a feeling in the pit of your stomach – that is a signal from your mind. Feelings from You influence you to go above and beyond, while feelings from your mind will aim to keep your body safe. Feelings from You are expanding; feelings from your mind are contracting.

Pausing for a bit to observe the feeling you're having in a particular moment will help you determine whether it comes from You or your mind. It will give you the time you need to analyze its source and decide to act on it or not. In the beginning it may seem like hard work, but as you do it more and more, your mind will learn to pause every time and act accordingly – it will become a new habit of your mind.

Whatever you bring up on the screen of your mind will be treated with a habitual reaction. If it's something or someone you love, a feeling of joy starts flooding your body. If it's something or someone who hurt you in the past, and your mind memorized the outcome, it will react in direct relation to the original feeling. So if you had a bad experience with a spider, a bat, a dog, a wasp, or whatever it was for you, whenever you bring that image on the screen of your mind, your whole body will be injected with a feeling of fear and contraction.

Take a moment right now to observe your feelings as you go through different scenarios. Like, for instance, there is something you want in your life. Disregard all of the reasons your mind starts throwing at you why you can't have it. Imagine that you have already achieved that something and you're about to enjoy it. What is your feeling telling you? If it's a feeling of excitement then that's bound to manifest quickly, and all you need to do is to act on it and go with the flow. If you must, put this book down and act on that feeling right now; take the very first step that you can make in the direction of your thought because a power bigger than your mind backs you up.

If, on the other hand, a feeling of fear starts overwhelming you and holds you back from acting, whether it's the fear of failure, the fear of criticism, the fear of rejection, or whatever kind of fear starts pumping adrenaline into your body, know that this is the reaction of your mind to this thought. Your mind can't create a scenario with the limited information it holds to "foresee" a possibility for you to achieve this dream, and not because it's impossible but because the mind itself can't see it. Acknowledge the feeling and keep telling yourself, "I am bigger than my mind," "I am bigger than my body," "I am a creator," "My mind is the executor of my will," "I am the master of my mind," "Whatever I want, my mind will find a way to make it possible," "My dream is possible," "My dream is achievable, and my mind will find a way to make it possible," and "My mind manifests anything I want to experience." Repeat these statements over and over until a feeling of confidence and assurance takes over, and then take action.

Don't act against your fear! Make the fear melt away with the feeling of confidence. Repeat these statements until your mind starts believing once again that its role is to execute your thoughts and understands that You are in charge. Once you reach that level of confidence that gives you the feeling of excitement when you think of your dream and goal, you can be sure that its manifestation is imminent and you can start acting toward achieving that goal.

Yes, it's true that most of the personal development gurus, speakers, and mentors will tell you to act in spite of your fear. Indeed, you can use the emotion of fear to fuel your desire, but the idea here is to control your mind, not your body, because we know that we have control over the body, and we can act on whatever we want. It's the mind that's holding us back on the journey. It's the mind that will trigger fearful thoughts along the way. It's the mind that You must master and control.

Preparing your mind is a tedious exercise and it requires perseverance, but You have to train the mind to be submissive to your will and make it believe that it can achieve anything for You to experience this life rather than "I have to protect this body at any cost." You aren't your body, and sooner or later, You're going to **decide** to give up this body. You decide how long this body survives on this planet.

There are no accidents. What we call accidents are mere experiences that the mind can't explain but that it's 100% responsible for. Our mind creates every situation and circumstance in our life. Our thoughts move the universe to manifestation. The more we dwell on a thought, the deeper it roots into our mind as a belief, and that belief is the root cause of the life we see around us.

For many years I earned my living from driving. Because **I became concerned I was** not **going to have proof** in case **of an accident**, I purchased a dash camera. My mind was at peace **now** that **every incident was being recorded**. I've put some words in bold because I want you to go back and read only those words again. What do you think happened after I installed my dash camera? I did indeed record every single incident. And the more I was focusing on those little incidents in the beginning, the bigger they got by the day, until one time I was literally a split of a second away from being hit "on camera."

That was the awakening moment when I realized that I had done this to myself by concerning myself with the accidents that might happen. I created those incidents! My thoughts manifested those incidents so I would have proof. And that was my proof that our thoughts manifest physically. That was the last time I used that dash camera. I decided to think that accidents won't happen to me, that I'm protected, and every time another incident happened (there were still some residual thoughts), I'd smile and feel gratitude for being safe. It's been ages since I've been anywhere near an accident; I can actually plan my journeys with no regard for possible incidents because **I don't think** about them. If I don't think about accidents, I don't create accidents. I drive relaxed because I know I always have safe journeys and always get to the destination on time.

Sometimes I have passengers with me whose thoughts and manifestations I can't control, but no matter what, I know I will be alright in the end. One time, my wife and I left home early in the morning heading to the airport for a vacation. For some reason she started becoming concerned whether we were going to make it in time, despite the fact I tried to assure her that we had plenty of time, and not long after that conversation, an accident caused the closure of the freeway less than a mile away from us. We were stranded there for almost an hour, but my confidence in the end result, the fact that we would board that plane no matter what, didn't shake for a second. We made it just in time.

Now, don't get me wrong; I don't blame her for "creating" that accident where people were involved. Whoever was involved in that accident created it, and my wife only sensed that accident happening. She couldn't explain the feeling that took over her body, but her mind released the fear anyway, and that thought and fear got us stuck in the queue.

Feelings for thoughts are like gas for fire, they accelerate the manifestation of said thoughts. Though the feeling came to her; it was merely an acknowledgement of an incident happening ahead of us. That feeling stirred thoughts like "Something happened" or "Something is going to happen." Because she didn't know what happened or would happen, her mind created more thoughts out of the fear of the unknown, so she, too, got involved in that particular accident by being stuck in the queue that formed behind it.

If you have ever had feelings like this that evolved into thoughts like that, know that you always have a choice in the matter of thoughts. In that moment, you can think that something amazing is about to happen, and you can use that boost to fuel the thoughts you want. Even though being stuck behind that accident couldn't probably have been prevented at that time, that fuel could have been used for something else other than worry. In the end nothing really happened – after all, we left home earlier specifically to account for "unforeseen" situations.

You have probably noticed that couples who have been together for decades, and loved each other deeply and cared for each other more than they did for themselves, form a special connection – a different kind of relationship. They no longer need words to communicate, they can sense each other's needs and wishes, and they can "foresee" each other's desires and misfortunes – like a set of identical twins.

This connection isn't random, but it's built on their love for each other, similar to that between a mother and her child. So after years of being together, having created this bridge that morphs them into one, when one of them decides to "leave" this world, for whatever reason (usually because they're sick and they **hate** being a burden to the other), the other one also "leaves" shortly after. They **feel** an emptiness within and they, too, decide to follow the other.

Most religious people insist on believing that God wants this, or God wants that. God allowed this. God permitted that. And then they look at the starvation, wars, hate, and jealousy and say that God allows that to happen for whatever "holy" reason. If you're a religious person, know this: "God is Love." God created humans with the gift of free will. Out of love, God gave us the greatest gift in the universe – creation – so we can create our own world and live as we please. Next time, when you think of blaming God for whatever reason, remember this: Your thoughts created the world you live in and your feelings watered the seeds of your ideas. God may be the creator of the universe, but You are the creator of the world in which you live, and if you don't like it, change it with your thoughts.

If you're thinking that natural calamities aren't our doing – think again! Do you remember the last insurance salesperson who tried to convince you to buy insurance from them for "n" reasons that "may" happen and you "could" experience? If an insurance company was aware of the damage it's doing, not to nature alone but to their own budget, by allowing these salespeople to put seeds of fear in the minds of their customers, they'd stop that right away.

Now imagine the millions of people who have been pitched to about all the natural disasters that "could" occur thinking of natural disasters. The best salespeople are those who make you think how you'd **feel** if something were to happen. Millions of thoughts spread all over the universe and empowered by feelings and emotions – that's bound to manifest somehow! When one little incident happens, and everybody sees it, thinks about it, and feels that sadness within for the people involved, it's like a dandelion clock that you blow into the air. Natural disasters, climate changes, hurricanes, etc. are all the result of our own thoughts, feelings, and actions.

The good part about having insurance, though, is the peace of mind that whatever is going to happen, you are protected financially, and when this kind of pitch is used by the salesperson, that is when the insurance company makes money – when they sell peace of mind.

When we watch the news and they show us all the disasters that are happening in the world, we think about them, and if we get emotionally involved, we give power to similar events. The media has no clue of the power of their actions when it presents the events. Moreover, some go through the trouble of editing and making the presentation even more dramatic because that's what attracts more ratings.

We can stop natural disasters and we can stop climate change, not by fighting it but by taking away its power. Stop thinking and talking about them. Buy your insurance for peace of mind and stop watching the news that depict disasters. It's the best way to protect the planet.

The best thing you can do for the people involved in disasters is to close your eyes, visualize the best outcome for their life, and share your love with them. Visualize yourself shifting their emotions, but don't let their emotions change yours. The second-best thing is to donate and support the charity or organization that deals with the situation.

If we change the channel from news about disasters to programs that show us the beauty of nature, the ratings will start shifting; the tragic news won't have views, while the programs about the beauty of nature will have growing numbers, and soon all channels will have to start presenting what "works" and brings more ratings. And the more programs about the beauty of nature, the more thoughts of beautiful nature will be in the minds of people, and the more thoughts of beautiful nature, the faster the manifestation will be. Even the news will shift from images of people cutting down trees to people planting them.

Chapter 5

BELIEF

Belief is the programming of the mind. It's the guiding system of our thoughts. It's the starting point for the creation of our thoughts, ideas, and eventually the things and events in our life. It's a state of acceptance of ideas. It's the foundation of our entire life.

A belief can be formed in four different ways: 1) by accepting the information provided by an authority, e.g. parents, teachers, churches, medics, governments, etc., 2) buying into the information of the masses, e.g. social media platforms, work culture, religious gatherings, business associations, etc., 3) by rationalizing the events and circumstances that happen around us daily, e.g.

deciding that the result in one event will be the same as with any similar upcoming events, and 4) by repetition of a statement over and over until it becomes a belief.

1) Trust in those with authority. Our parents, or tutors, are those who built the foundation of our paradigm from which we absorbed our first beliefs and are also the ones to whom we'd, generally, go for guidance first as they're the early faces we've seen as children, and by nature we trust them the most. A parent isn't only the guide of a new mind, it is also the icon, and the goal of aspiration. As they introduce us to teachers for further education, we gain their trust also. If the family goes to a church, a synagogue, a temple, a mosque, etc., it introduces the new mind to another authority that can be trusted because the parents trust it. The government is also an established authority in creating new laws for the benefit of all. Any of the above authorities, on different levels, have an influence over our beliefs: what we eat, how we dress, what we say and when, what we learn, who or what the superhuman being is that gives us power and guidance, and who we listen to for the benefit of the nation.

2) Buying into the information of the masses. Whether this kind of information starts in the form of a factual discovery of an individual or an

assumption, it spreads from one ear to another as it grows in power by the number of people who hear it and pass it on – the more people who talk about one piece of information, the more power it gains and becomes less shakeable. Social media is one of the mediums through which this kind of information is spread around. When reading about it multiple times, the mind accepts it as true. If you go to a place of work, that company may have a specific vision, which implies a specific belief that helps it head that way. A religious gathering also has a powerful effect on the belief of an individual. The most common thought that comes to mind when buying into this is "If so many people say so, it must be true."

3) Rationalizing the events and circumstances that happen around us daily. A powerful mind is one that does its own thinking. Though, still influenced by the information stored from childhood, environment, and other emotional creeds, the mind analyzes the events on its own and draws its own beliefs. It evolves out of trust or distrust for authorities, or simply out of curiosity.

4)The repetition of a statement over and over until it impregnates into the mind. If you hear something over and over for long enough, your mind reaches the belief point. Whether it is a good thing or not, the repeated information becomes the creed of the mind. Soldiers are told a "particular" story and given a "particular" reason to fight for their country – some we call heroes, while others we call terrorists. The process of becoming that is exactly the same. This doesn't relate to what we hear alone but also to what we consciously tell ourselves. A made-up story in our mind repeated over and over becomes a vivid memory as if the individual has experienced it at some point in the past – this is why people "remember" different scenarios of the same event.

None of the above ways to implement a belief in one's mind are good or bad. They're just ways through which the mind can be influenced. Positive or negative information can be passed on to the mind through any one of these ways. A deaf child born with no ears can be acknowledged as a "normal" one, and his mutism transformed into an advantage for a successful life (Hill, 2007, chapter 2: Desire Outwits Mother Nature – in which the author tells the story of his own boy).

In the beginning, our mind accepts everything that is given "in faith." As we didn't have a module through which to "filter" and sort out the thoughts, our mind accepted everything as it was given. A parent will say to their child: "If you eat all your dinner, you'll grow tall," "If you dress nicely, people will like you more," or "If you do well at school, you'll have a great career," and the child accepts these statements as facts and starts building their judgement on them. As the child grows, wanders, and discovers new "facts," some will match their beliefs and some won't. Those facts that create conflict force the mind to rationalize and weigh the options to choose one or the other, or even both to be used in different contexts.

Repetition of a statement over and over for a period of time can override previous statements and change beliefs. This is similar to overriding a program in a computer, though this process is a bit more tedious, any belief can be replaced at will with any other chosen one.

If your belief is one or more of these: "I have to work hard to earn money," "I have to stop eating to lose weight," or "I have to be lucky to find a good partner," you could change it to "Money is coming to me easily and effortlessly," "I have a lean and healthy body regardless of what I eat," or "I attract into my life the perfect match for my character," and you can do that by repeating these statements over and over until your mind accepts them and starts acting accordingly. There is a good point often raised that the new statements aren't "realistic." My question is: "They aren't realistic according to whose reality?"

We all create in our minds our own reality, which is based on personal experiences. If we all lived in the same reality, we'd never have any reasons to argue or fight. There would be no wars, no starvation, and no homeless people. There would be no cultural differences. The reality of one would be the reality of all and vice-versa. So next time someone asks you to be realistic, remember that they refer to their own reality, and when you ask someone else to be realistic, you will be talking about the reality in which you believe, in which your mind is comfortable. Your mind will search for things to relate to in what you're hearing from others and will only connect with them on that level.

Your reality isn't your neighbor's reality. The reality of a healthy person is different from the reality of a sick person. The reality of the rich is different from the reality of the poor. The difference is in what each individual believes to be their reality, and every individual has the capability to change their reality by changing their belief – by changing the stories and statements they tell themselves and others.

To change your reality, you have to change your paradigm, your belief system, and you can do this using affirmations. The word affirmation comes from the Latin *affirmare*, originally meaning "to make steady, to strengthen." Affirmations are proven methods of self-improvement because of their ability to rewire our brains. Much like exercise, they raise the level of feel-good hormones and push our brains to form new clusters of thought neurons. Affirmations break patterns of thoughts, speech, and actions.

There's a specific way to reprogram your mind using affirmations, otherwise you may actually get the opposite effect. For instance, your mind doesn't perceive negation. We use negation in our day-to-day speech to revert the effect of an action: "Do you want this?" "I don't want this!" The mind doesn't work that way, its focus is on the main words "I" – the subject, "want" – the action, "this" – the thing to be obtained. So if you're tired of a relationship and want to end it and say a statement like "I don't want this relationship," your mind records "**I don't want this relationship**."

"Why?" you may ask. Well, if you imagine the programming in a computer or smartphone, you can't command your computer or smartphone not to open a new page or application – "I don't want to open this page" (while clicking on it). If you don't want to open it, you simply don't click on it. The computer will execute every command you give, ignoring the negation. Here is a little exercise: if you want to have some fun with Siri, Cortana,

Google, Alexa, or any other artificial intelligence, give them a negative command – "Don't play this" or "Don't open that" – and see what happens.

The existing programming also plays a vital role in the interpretation of your affirmations. A statement like "I will be rich" implies that you aren't rich in this moment and that is the core belief that dominates your subconscious mind, and the manifestation of your belief keeps you in the same state. Though on the other hand, it can be used as a transitioning affirmation to allow your mind to adapt to the new belief that it is possible for you to become rich, and it becomes the driver for your actions toward your goal. Most of us don't know how our mind has been programmed, especially if we have done nothing conscious to train it, so a very effective way to achieve the belief that you desire is to follow these simple rules when creating affirmations:

– Always start with "I" because it's You who is living in the body and has the power to control and reprogram the mind.

– Always use the present tense because You only live now: "I am," "I know," "I see," "I believe," etc. You can emphasize on the present by adding the word "now": "I am now," "I now know," "I now see," "I now believe," etc.

– Always use the words that describe what you want to achieve instead of what you don't want. A statement like "I now lose fat" won't have the desired effect because the word "fat" triggers on the screen of your mind the image that you don't want, but that is the image commanded, while the word "lean" shows and commands exactly what you want to achieve.

– Always focus on the end result as if you've already achieved it. Forget about "Isn't this a lie?" This isn't a social contract; this is mind reprogramming! If you want a great relationship, use something like "I am now in the best relationship." If you want better health, say, "I am now in the best shape ever," or if you want more money, say, "I now have more than enough money to buy anything I want."

I agree that it may sound like a lie when making these statements, but know that it only sounds like a lie to your mind because it contradicts with the information it has perceived through its senses. If you are surrounded by a big wall, your mind can't tell you what's behind it because it can't see anything behind it and can't hear anything, and it will always hold you back from going over. But You **know** that behind it is freedom.

That wall is, metaphorically speaking, your mind's limitation. Your brain can only work with the information that it perceives through its senses or what you give to it through imagination by creating pictures on the screen of your mind. That means you can only go behind that wall if you can see yourself in your imagination behind it, and if you show your mind that there is something there worth going for.

On the other hand, your mind, through its programming, may bring up images it has recorded in the past in an attempt to hold you back. This is why children are fearless – they don't have any images recorded by their mind to show them; all they have is faith and curiosity.

So by creating images of what you want to have or be, You are reprogramming your mind by bringing new information to the table – a new truth; the one that You want in your life. You are unlimited. You are abundance. You are health. You are prosperity. You are what You are! This is the information that you bring, and that you feed to your mind for it to manifest into the physical world – to create.

Beliefs are much stronger than thoughts in the process of manifestation because they have been created through repetitive thoughts of the same nature. If you believe the only way to earn money is to work for someone else, the thought of being your own boss will be dismissed by your mind in an instant, which only gives the manifestation of your thought a very slim chance. So a change of belief is necessary to be able to surface the actual thoughts you want to manifest.

Questioning the baseline of your belief is what starts shaking it. For instance, you can say, "Okay, if the only way to earn money is by working for someone else, who is my boss working for?" and this way, going up in the command chain, you'll realize that at the top there is this one person who responds to nobody – the big boss, the creator, and the one who envisioned the business. They have more money than any of those working for them and yet nobody is handing them a monthly or weekly paycheck.

From this point you can make a parallel with yourself; what do they have that you don't? Your mind will show you pictures of the end result. But only what it can perceive through its senses and because there is no story to that end result: how they got there, to be at the top of the ladder – the comparison seems impossible and frightening. If further questioning is applied, your mind will then attempt to explain it through whatever images it has in store. If that storage has only images from gangster movies in which the big boss had to kill and oppress others to get to the top, you may think that's probably not what you want to do to reach that level. Your belief will dissipate any chance your thought may have had for you to become the big boss.

If the movies you've watched or the books you've read were biographies of people who started from the same level you are on right now, or below, and worked their way up, your belief about the big boss will be of a hard-working individual with a vision who achieved it – now this looks like something you can do, right? This is a belief that doesn't contradict the morals and a belief that will support your thought of being your own boss.

So if you want to be your own boss, but you don't know how to do it, start reading biographies of successful people. How many? Well, that depends on how strong the belief is you want to change; it may take one book that you may relate to, or it may take 100 from which your mind may harvest what it needs. In doing so, you are reprogramming your mind by feeding it new information and new images that will help it see new possibilities.

You don't always need the conviction of your mind, but as it's your best supporter and helper you may want to have it on your side, otherwise it may sabotage your plans and slow You down in the process. You are powerful enough to do and be anything You want.

Imagine that you decide to quit your job and become your own boss but your mind isn't "formed" for an entrepreneurial life. Almost everything that you build in a day, your brain will dismantle overnight, and the next day you'll have to start over; at some point it's going to be a battle of persistence. This is why all the mentors, coaches, and trainers tell you that persistence, even though it's not a bold characteristic, is absolutely essential for success.

But you don't have to fight your mind; you have to get it on your side – on the side of your goal – the same way it's been trained to be. You can train it to be what You want it to be, and together you may live happily ever after. Just pick whatever goal You want to achieve, and write down on paper all the reasons why you should have that, and all the reasons for which you deserve it. In the process of writing, you involve the physical senses through which your brain picks the information. Once written down, You should also read it out loud for the same reason. Do it in front of a mirror and it becomes even more powerful.

When writing down and reading out loud, do it from a position of power – You are the master. You are the power that makes it possible. You aren't talking to your mind; you're stating those things because they're the new truth, and your mind is but a witness to your new statement. You don't need its permission to have or be what you want – just lay down Your plan and inform it of the new path. Part two of the process is to become one with the wish You desire.

You are energy and You can take the form of anything by choice. When you were born on this planet, there were no previous broadcasted messages sent from your station. Once the mind starts working, messages are being sent; if the body needs food, the mind creates the message, sends it out, and food is supplied.

As your mind evolved and started perceiving the physical world, new thoughts were born; you discovered your hands and fingers, you put them in your mouth, tasted them, and felt them. The same with your feet and toes. Then as your eyes started developing, shiny and colorful objects appeared in the distance, and the thought of reaching them popped into your mind. In the beginning there wasn't much correlation between your mind and limbs, but as you discovered what each of them was doing and how you could use them to your advantage to get you closer to your desired object, you started crawling and eventually reached your aim. With a bit of imagination, you can see where I'm going with this. All the thoughts that were created in your mind, very basic and simple in the beginning, were eventually manifested.

Then something else stirred your interest – the people around you: parents, siblings, tutors, etc. You saw them eating with a spoon, and you wanted that too; you saw them walking on two feet, and you aimed for that too; you wanted to experience everything they were doing, but then something happened – you saw them walking down the stairs, but somehow you weren't allowed. You really didn't understand why they were stopping you, so on the next occasion, you tried again, but every time they saw you, they stopped you. Then one day, when no one was around, you tried one more time, and for obvious reasons, you fell and hurt yourself. So then, in that little mind of yours, a correlation is made, and with the help of emotion, a belief has been created. Not enough, though, to stop you from trying something else, but with every new thing that those who try to protect you and stop you from doing proves to be true, trust begins to form, and with every new thing engaged emotionally, a new belief is being born to lay down the foundation of your existence.

Now, on a new level of thinking, you concluded that their words were words of wisdom, so you listened to them, more or less. As your mind grew stronger, it wanted to absorb more and more information. With your strong senses you could see them from a distance, and you could hear them when they were talking, even though you were playing. All that information was stored in your mind, and whether they were showing love to each other or fighting, with the emotion involved in those actions, new beliefs were created in your little mind.

Some children are born or adopted into rich families where the general state of being is that most things are affordable as long as there is money. To make plenty of money, it is required of them to aim for a highly paid career or go into business for themselves, just as they saw in their home from an early life, and when they go to school, their mind takes them on the path that's formed deep within. Some children, even though they are born into rich families, perceive life as being offered on a platter because most of the things they wanted had been offered ahead of them asking, or shortly after with little or no tantrum. Their general state of belief is "I can do anything I want and if things go south, my parents will fix it."

Some children are born into poverty with parents who work hard for every penny, some are born into "broken families," some are abandoned altogether, and so on. The more you think of it, the more categories you discover.

The idea is that the family, the environment in which an individual is raised, serves as basic information for establishing their beliefs.

My parents worked very hard to offer me and my little siblings a "decent" life. And they realized that in order for us to live an easier life than they had, we would have to follow a path toward a career that would offer us that, so when I was fourteen, I went to a boarding school.

Living day and night with young adults of my age or older, from a vast variety of backgrounds, all my beliefs that I had formed in my years living with my parents were shattered to pieces within a year of living there. The second year, my mind worked on forming new beliefs that would serve as bridges between the two worlds I was living in – home and school. In the third year, I concluded that the path I was on wasn't what I wanted, and I started paying less and less attention to the path the majority of my classmates were on and focused more and more on the options I could do instead.

Throughout the five years I lived in that school, I transformed myself into a completely new individual. The environment played the biggest role in my transformation. With a new perception of the world, I formed new beliefs. With new beliefs, the world I was living in had changed.

After the five years elapsed, I embarked on a journey to discover myself. Moving from home and changing the environment, subconsciously I made myself believe that this was what I needed in order to find myself, as if I were a piece of a puzzle traveling across the board to find my unique spot. I moved across the country, and as planned in my mind, on my first day there, I found myself both a place to live and my first paid job.

Little did I know at the time, my confidence, and the belief I had in my ability to find these two, played the most important role, though I'd never looked for a place to rent or been to a job interview before then. The universe arranged itself to match my thoughts – the plans I'd created in my mind in which I believed. Sometimes we think that we need a strong belief in order to achieve something. The truth is that faith has no levels – we either believe or not. And when we believe, we feel it with our whole being, and we **know** it to be true. On the other hand, when we want to believe in something, that kind of hopeful outcome, that's not belief; that's wishful thinking. It's an attempt of our mind to see a possible outcome, but not a conviction in its realization.

Four years later, something was still missing; I didn't seem to be in the spot I was meant to fit in. My high school love, with whom I maintained the relationship, moved to study in a different city, so I moved once more, hoping that maybe my place was near someone I loved – another piece of the puzzle with an edge that fits with mine.

With the same plan I had four years back, I started looking for a job. This time it didn't happen the first day, or the first week, or month. I applied to all the jobs that I could find – if only I could get an interview. Something was missing from the equation and I couldn't figure out what it was. Why was the last time straightforward and this time wasn't?

But the universe has a different way of arranging itself than what we imagine with our minds. So after three months, and a mountain of debt, I found this lady who had a licensed taxi and needed a driver. She agreed to let me drive her car, even though I didn't have a taxi license, and I gave up looking for a job. Every day I'd drive on the road, hoping someone would get in and show me the way to their destination as the town was new to me and I didn't have much knowledge of its streets.

I had a taxi radio and found myself some maps to aid me. While waiting for the next client to get in my cab, I was listening the other drivers taking bookings and searching the map to find their locations and the addresses they were going to, and all this with my eyes on the lookout for people from the council who were roaming the city in search of unlicensed drivers like myself.

Months later, though I hadn't applied for a job since I started driving the taxi, my desire to get myself a "proper job" sprang out, and one day, out of the blue, I received a phone call from an agency that said they had a job interview for me as a salesperson for a renowned car dealership. It was my first interview since I'd moved here. I was so excited; I called my fiancée right away to tell her the big news.

The missing piece in the original plan was the attachment to the outcome. Once I let go of my narrow-minded way of doing things and allowed the universe to express itself, I got what I was looking for.

I went to the interview totally unprepared. All I had was the belief that the job was mine – I knew in my heart this job was mine and there was no doubt about it. It turned out the position wasn't for me to sell the popular brand but one I had only heard about in races. That didn't stop me though – I wanted the job. After a long series of technical questions like "What is the difference between a diesel engine and a petrol one?" all of which I failed, I sarcastically asked if the position was for a mechanic!

When we got to the wages, he explained that there was a basic salary plus commission from sales. Then he asked me what my expectation was for the basic salary. My answer was "I don't care about that. Tell me more about the commission." I knew that the basics wouldn't change much, but if I could sell more cars, I would get more money.

"Well," he replied, "you'll get 0.4% of the value of the car you sell."

"Great!" I said, "What if I sell more cars?"

"How many?" he asked.

"Five …?"

"If you sell five cars in one month, I'll give you 0.5%."

"Great!" I said excitedly, "What if I sell ten cars in a month?" At this point I felt that he had become uncomfortable.

"If you sell ten cars in a month, I'll give you one percent," came his abrupt answer.

I was super excited, and I believe he saw that in my eyes. He felt this energy glowing from my body because except for his curiosity to see if I could really do what I said, nothing else in that interview went well, though he gave me the job. It was a few weeks later, after I started the job, when I found out that the one-man team who was in the showroom sold only five cars the previous year, and he was excited about having sold six already in the first nine months of that year when I joined. "They're not as known as the popular brands," was his argument.

We went on to sell twelve more cars in the last quarter. In March I reached my first "five cars a month" goal, and in June I exceeded my ten cars goal and delivered a total of twenty-seven. It's amazing what we can achieve when we put our minds to it – without the limitations of our society. If I had known they only sold eleven cars in twenty-one months, do you think my mind would've dared to dream of aiming for ten cars in a month? Most probably not, but in my clueless mind, where no limitations have been set yet by the environment, I was able to see it was possible. I believed with my heart and desired it with my whole being. The universe answered to my faith and delivered the physical manifestation of my thoughts, not as I had wished but almost three times over.

Belief is the very core of our existence. It's that which allows us to stand up – if you don't believe you can stand up, you won't even bother to try to stand up. Belief is that which makes it possible for us to walk, talk, eat, and drink. How many times have you heard people saying, "Oh, I don't believe

I can do that," as an excuse for not trying? They believe to be incapable of whatever it is they don't do. There are countless examples of people who walked after they suffered terrible injuries in accidents, despite the fact that doctors gave them no physical chance. There are countless people who bent the laws of nature because they believed. What we call miracles are only miracles for the faithless minds.

Those "miracles" are in fact the direct response of belief. Sometimes it takes a split second, sometimes it takes three months for its manifestation. On a daily basis there are still people healing diseases in their bodies taking sugar pills (placebo) instead of actual treatment because they believe that they can get better. They believe in miracles. They simply believe.

Society has educated us in such a way that we can only believe something if we see it. We refuse categorically to believe certain things because our mind can't explain them; our limited mind doesn't have the necessary information to create that picture to show us that it's possible. For ages, humanity believed that thunder and lightning were some sort of wrath of the gods. For ages, humanity believed the earth was flat – until someone didn't. It only took one person to believe differently for the entire world to change, and once that person found a way to physically prove it, the rest of the world was able to believe as well.

> Our housekeeping is mendicant, our arts, our occupations, our marriages, our religion, we have not chosen, but society has chosen for us. We are parlour soldiers. We shun the rugged battle of fate, where strength is born. (Emerson, 2017, p. 68)

We allow ourselves to believe that we are a product of the society we live in, and we are, because that is what we believe. Only when we find the power to detach ourselves from the culture of the society, we find the power within, we discover the uniqueness of our being and the power to create a life by design.

> *"If you believe it will work out, you'll see opportunities. If you believe it won't, you'll see obstacles." —Wayne Dyer*

> *"Believe in yourself. Know that there is something inside you that is greater than any obstacle." — Christian D. Larson*

> *"For those who believe, no proof is necessary. For those who don't believe, no proof is possible." — Stuart Chase*

"The future belongs to those who believe in the beauty of their dreams." —Eleanor Roosevelt "

All things are possible for those who believe." —Jesus Christ

"You are what you believe yourself to be" —Paulo Coelho

"I am the greatest, I said that even before I knew I was." — Muhammad Ali

"Belief creates the actual fact." — William James

Belief is the seed of the thought. The ideas that have been passed on to us by society are those that we believe to be true and what makes our life what it is. For us to be able to live a different life, we must choose different thoughts. By changing our beliefs, we change the type of thoughts we create. When we have changed a belief, new thoughts spring into our mind and those thoughts are the preview of our future life.

Chapter 6

UNIVERSAL CONSCIOUSNESS

We spoke in the second chapter that what we call the conscious is actually You manifesting into the physical world, and the subconscious is the mind itself – the software of the brain. So here is a question: Where is You coming from?

Minds all over the world, since the beginning of time, have sensed the presence of You in their body mostly through inexplicable things and have attempted to describe You based on the things and circumstances that surrounded the event. To this day, You has been described as a good god, a bad god, an old god, a wise god, a dual god, a triad of gods, a reign of gods, a higher self, a spirit, a soul, etc., and that surely explains the number of religions across the world throughout time.

People have fought each other for millennia in the name of their god, believing either that their god is the only true god or stronger than the other's. In reality, each of the gods described were but simple projections of people's minds. We look back in history to the myths that once were foundations of belief for past societies, and it makes us chuckle when we think of their naivety, not even realizing that whatever we believe right now is but another projection of our mind that uses new information and could equally be a reason to giggle for the minds of the future.

The mind, limited by the knowledge accumulated in its lifetime, knows only what it sees with its eyes, feels with its physical senses, and hears with its ears – a skilled teller could easily create a believable picture for the mind to roll on its screen. But the biggest downside of the mind is that it fears what it can't see, hence the power that some religions have over the minds of their followers – claiming that if one doesn't follow its rules they will burn in hell for eternity. We received most of the information we have from our families and society, and we pass this on to the future generations as the truth by which we live our lives, whether we lived it ourselves or we have accepted it as it was given to us.

Each generation discovers new truths and adds this to the story they pass on – making the truth variable. A variable truth makes a variable life. If you ever look at the way your parents lived, and their parents before them, you will realize that your life is totally different, and this wouldn't have been possible without their input. Some made judgement errors, but that's fine because the whole of humanity did the same throughout history, and without the errors, they wouldn't have discovered the new truth.

Less than two hundred years ago people feared lightning. When science discovered the process through which lightning is created and how it moves, they were able to determine where it was more likely to appear, and they built lightning conductors (rods) and placed them on top of high buildings; therefore, controlling and directing the "wrath of God" away from people and their houses. Once the mind understands the process, it no longer fears it.

As the mind learned more and more about the trigger of fear that dominates most of the religions of the world, it changed our attitude toward religion. Once humans discovered that they could control other fellow humans with fear, they traveled the world and spread the word of their own powerful projected god who could easily crush its enemies; therefore, spreading fear amongst them. People have been asked to bring offerings and sacrifices to their gods to keep them happy. People have been told to follow the rules or they will burn for eternity. But the fear used in religions all over the world can only control the mind.

There are over 30,000 gods known to have been worshipped (Hill, 2007). In other words, there are over 30,000 ways the mind has described You. Today, some minds are so narrowly focused on their own projection and blinded by their ego that they refuse to "see" the same being expressed in different forms and shapes all over the world. Some are so confused and overwhelmed by the information that they refuse to believe altogether that such beings exists. Some of the scientists, on the other hand, believe to have the answers to the creation of the universe; therefore, eliminating a god altogether from the equation and leaving it to chaos.

We are all connected both physically and spiritually; in essence we come from the same source. The energy of You is the same energy that makes the acorn an oak tree, a larvae into a butterfly, or an egg into a bird. The same energy that makes your heart beat also makes the trees grow. When this energy leaves a tree, the tree goes into a process of material disintegration, and the same happens with any other living body. In the words of the great Antoine Lavoisier, describing the natural law of conservation of mass, we understand we are all one: "In nature, nothing is created, nothing is destroyed, but everything is transformed."

The ancient Sanskrit text of Shvetashvatara Upanishad explains that, "God, who is one only, is hidden in all beings. He is all-pervading, and is the inner self of all creatures. He presides over all actions, and all beings reside in Him. He is the witness, and He is the Pure Consciousness." (YouSigma, 2008, VI-11)

For thousands of years we have known that we are all connected, but for the mind this had to have a specific meaning, a physical connection, so it reduced its significance to bloodlines, local communities, race, and religion. We now hear people saying, "We are family," or "We have to protect our own," or "We are one in Christ." Whichever statement you've heard or used in the past only diminishes the magnitude of oneness. The mind is too small to see it all, but You only have to open your eyes to see. You are in all that is connected to You. You create with your thoughts and attract into your world all that is in it – You are the link to it all.

If you isolate a plant into a pot, ignore it, and forget to water it, it will wither. But if you put in the pot some composted organic matter and water it regularly, it will thrive. If you talk to it and love it (still a form of energy), it will grow even quicker. What happens to your body if you don't feed it? The same thing that happens with any other body or plant. This is a primordial way of absorbing energy; it's still necessary though, until such time as we have evolved enough to live off love alone.

The mind, by design, seeks to grade, organize, weigh, and measure. That's why there are minds that think there are different energies in plants and different energies in animals. The core reason being that the mind can't accept the idea of consuming itself. If all life on Earth is one, by the act of eating, one eats itself. For a mind that is limited in understanding, such a thing is unacceptable; therefore, it creates a theory – a belief – in which it can live without being labelled cannibalistic.

Once you separate the mind from energy, from You, the mere act of eating is but material. The energy doesn't need to feed on something; it merely needs a conductor to move itself from one form into another. You aren't your mind and You aren't your body. You are the life that flows through your body and makes the existence of your mind possible.

As mentioned previously in this book, You are the conscious and your mind is the subconscious. Up until now people have talked about conscious and subconscious as two parts of the mind, which if you think about it, once life leaves the body, both should cease to exist. However, the assumption we're making here is that the conscious – life, energy, or the spirit; You – is not limited by the mass of our body, the knowledge of our mind, or the number of times this planet revolves around the sun.

So when I'm quoting other authors, keep in mind this distinction, not because they aren't right in what they're saying but because they are – they feel the difference, and they know the difference; they're simply using a different terminology.

Back to You – if this energy never dies but only flows through matter giving it the animation that we call life, it means that the same energy that is in me, as I'm writing this, is also in you reading it. Consider this book a form of energy that enriches your intellect the same way the plants and animals we eat give us the energy we need to use our bodies. You, and me, and the nature that surrounds us are all connected through this one energy manifested in different forms.

The sun gives us a form of energy, the water gives us another form of energy, a song may give us that "feel good" energy, a piece of art gives us that "peace and wonder" energy, and love gives us joyful energy. Think about it; as we described in the fourth chapter, if we increase the level of vibration of ice it becomes water and then steam, sound, radio wave, microwaves, heat, red, ultraviolet, X-ray and finally thought. The same energy on different levels of vibration becomes something else; however, it's still the same energy.

This means we are all connected through the same energy; we live in the same energy as the same energy. We are all one. So when you hear or read Mike Dooley's famous quote, "Thoughts become things... choose the good ones!®," (©www.tut.com) you will know that this is true because your thoughts can take the form of anything by simply changing its level of vibration.

Also, if we are all connected, it means we can all feel and we can communicate with nature and with each other, and we do, even though most of the time we're looking for physical explanations rather than simply accepting the fact. A bee will sting you if it senses fear, a dog will come to your aid if it feels you're in danger, and a loved one will hug you when you feel sad and will laugh with you when you are happy. We are connected through these "vibes" we feel in each other and we are connected in thought also. My wife and I discovered that, sometimes, the phone is less efficient than our connection. I was shopping one day and sent her a text asking what kind of pizza to get; because she took longer than usual to reply I just chose one. Later her text came through asking for exactly the one I had already got. Coincidence? Maybe ... Another day my brother asked me to do some shopping for a barbeque. He gave me a list and, on top of it, I added two more items: corn on the cob and halloumi. When I got to his place, his wife said, "I wanted to ask you to get some corn on the cob and haloumi, but your brother told me you're already on your way back, so I didn't call," – again, coincidence? I could list hundreds of examples, but you already know this to be true because you've experienced it too, but you've only assumed it must be a coincidence.

If the information moves from my wife to me, or my sister-in-law to me, through this unknown frequency, it means that anyone can pick up this information if they tune in on our frequency, by chance or on purpose. It also means that anyone can tune in on anyone's frequency.

More often than we care to admit, we emulate the people we admire in an attempt to replicate their results – more like an instinct. Somewhere deep within, we know there's a process of what we have to do in order to obtain whatever results we want, but our mind doesn't know the process. Our mind does what it can the best way possible, and if sometimes you can't replicate the results of others, don't beat yourself up because your mind did its best – it just hasn't been trained properly; but if you want, you can retrain your mind over and over until you get the results you seek.

The actual process shouldn't be the mind's emulation of other people's actions but You tuning in on the frequency of what you desire and want to manifest. When you see someone rich, it's because their You is on that particular frequency of manifestation of riches, and if you want similar riches, you don't have to take it from them, and you don't have to do what they did – you only have to tune in on the frequency of riches and manifest them into your life and both of you can be rich. The same applies to love, health, and whatever it is that you want for your experience.

When this idea first came to me, my mind was, like, *so … if anyone in this world wants to be rich, they can? Where are all those riches going to come from? The villas, the cars, the boats, the clothes, the jewels, etc.?* I remembered from history lessons that humanity hasn't always lived in houses and apartment buildings, didn't always drive cars, and so on. They first lived in caves, until one came up with an idea to build a covering outside the cave, and when others saw that, they built one as well. One even thought of moving the covering away from the cave and adding walls, and then they all did the same; then one thought of adding windows, and then they all did the same. Can you see where I'm going with this? By creating a physical item or idea from imagination, we plant images of that in the minds of others.

When Henry Ford drove his horseless carriage on the streets of Detroit for the first time, he planted the seed of imagination in the minds of other people to see themselves driving one as well. There was a time when only the richest people could afford to drive a car, or have a TV set in their home, or own a mobile phone. Whatever people called riches 100 years ago, they're no longer that, and whatever we call riches now, in 100 years they won't be that.

If you want riches, you don't have to wait a century for them to be made accessible to you; you have to learn to tune in on the frequency of what you want, and to see yourself in your imagination already in possession of what you want. It took humanity decades to own a car because they didn't dare to see themselves in their mind owning that car. People have had their minds so cluttered by "how" that they didn't even try to imagine themselves in that position. It had to be a new generation of uncluttered minds, children who had no limitation imposed in their minds, to play with their imagination and see themselves as what they will become.

If you want a happy relationship, you don't have to go and steal anyone's partner in the hope that they will make you happy. You only have to tune in on the frequency of the happiness that you see in others; be happy for them, and on that frequency, you will find the partner who matches your frequency.

If you want good health, tune in on the health frequency. Sickness and disease are nothing but frequencies and we only get them because we don't know we are on the wrong frequency. Once you learn to make out the difference between the sickness frequency and the health frequency, you will know how to tune in on the one you want. Have you, as a kid or otherwise, tried to skip school or work and had all sorts of thoughts that led to events that made your wish possible? Just think about it! You've created events with your thoughts that led to the manifestation of your wish. If you lied to your teacher or your boss and told them you were sick, very shortly after you actually became sick, similarly if, despite your sickness, you wished to go to school or work, you soon made that sickness disappear.

Whatever it is that you want already exists, and it has a frequency in the universal consciousness. All you have to do is to tune in on that frequency and be it. The way to achieve this is through your imagination. The mind doesn't make out the difference between the information received through its physical senses and the information planted by You. Your mind takes in faith the information it receives from parents, teachers, government, religious leaders, etc. We believe stories that have been told to us, so what's stopping us believing stories that we tell us?

Exercise: go into a quiet room, sit in a comfortable position, close your eyes, and take deep breaths and relax until you feel yourself sinking into the chair or couch. Observe the thoughts and images that show on the screen of your mind like you're browsing different channels on your TV set; each channel is on a different frequency. Now, consciously pick a frequency that you want – a channel that shows you what you want in your life, what you want to be, do, or have. See yourself as the main character in this new movie you've tuned in to, and allow yourself to be happy, wealthy, or healthy, and enjoy life on the screen of your mind as if you already have what you want. Engage your emotions and feel whatever it is that you want with all your body. You are now tuned in on the frequency of what you want, and because you tuned in on this frequency, the universe starts to rearrange itself to bring to you the things, places, and people required to manifest that image, "or something better" – as Mike Dooley says – in the physical world.

Your mind may not be properly formed to bring these images to you in one sitting, but if every day, or every so often, you take a moment from your busy life to simply visualize the life you want, you will have eventually created that channel of manifestation that brings to you the things you want.

You can think of universal consciousness as a database of information available to all who want to tune in with their own printing machine – the mind – and print them in the physical world. If you want to hang on a wall an image of your favorite place, you can go on your computer, search the internet, and find the picture you want; you can bring it up on the screen of your computer, tablet, or smartphone that is connected to a printer and select print. The picture that was virtually on your computer is now physically in your hands. The universal consciousness isn't the World's Wide

Web; it's the Universe's Wide Web, where all the pictures that the mind can prints exist. And because for You there is no time, whatever the mind calls past or future is all in one place for You.

Thomas Edison saw the image of a city illuminated by artificial light while browsing the Universe's Wide Web and brought it to life by making the lightbulb possible. Henry Ford saw an image of faster transportation across the world and brought to life the mass production of cars. The Wright brothers saw images of the earth from above and brought to life the plane. Bill Gates saw a computer in every home; Elon Musk saw electric transportation and Mars colonization; and I saw this book and put it in writing. None of these people are the creators of their ideas – they are but the ones who manifested them into the physical world through their burning desire.

The proof of this is all of the ideas that came to your mind that you've never acted on and then later saw manifested. The images of the mobile phones I saw when I was a kid, and the electric cars, already existed. It was just a matter of time before someone took advantage of the existing picture and brought it into the physical realm.

Traian Vuia, a Romanian inventor, applied for and received a patent for a flying machine only six months before the Wright Brothers made their first successful take off (Wikipedia), which is proof that a picture of a flying device was in the minds of many. The fact that only a few believed in the idea and went on to work to materialize it is the everlasting dilemma of humanity because many see but only a few choose to believe.

Dr. Joe Vitale (2014), in his book The Secret to Attracting Money, tells a story about an idea for a DVD product that came to his mind. He acted on his thoughts along with a friend in the backyard of his estate, and during the recordings, another friend called and left him a voicemail saying that he just had this amazing idea and wanted to know if he'd be willing to work together on it – it was exactly the same idea that Dr. Joe Vitale was filming in that very moment.

Dr. Elmer R. Gates created more than 200 patents by deliberately connecting to the Universe's Wide Web and bringing the ideas on paper. He had what he called a "personal communication room" – a soundproof and lightproof room with a small table on which he kept a pad of paper for writing. Whenever he wanted to search for images and ideas for his inventions, he'd go into this room, switch off the lights, and concentrate until what he was looking for started flashing into his mind. Then he'd switch on the light and start writing. On one occasion, ideas came through so abundantly that he wrote for three hours. (Hill, 2007)

Napoleon Hill, in his book *Think and Grow Rich*, when talking about the mind said,

> The faculty of creative imagination is the direct link between the finite mind of man and Infinite Intelligence. All so-called revelations, referred to in the realm of religion, and all discoveries of basic or new principles in the field of invention, take place through the faculty of creative imagination.
>
> When ideas or concepts flash into one's mind, through what is popularly called a "hunch," they come from one or more of the following sources:
>
> 1) Infinite Intelligence
>
> 2) One's subconscious mind, wherein is stored every sense impression and thought impulse which ever reached the brain through any of the five senses
>
> 3) From the mind of some other person who has just released the thought, or picture of the idea or concept, through conscious thought, or
>
> 4) From another person's subconscious storehouse.
>
> There are no other **known** [bold added for emphasis] sources from which "inspired" ideas or "hunches" may be received. (Hill, 2007)

Let's dive into these sources for a bit:

1) Infinite Intelligence, or the universal consciousness, is the database of past, present, and future ideas and information; it is the storehouse of everything – the National Grid or the World Wide Web of the universe. No matter how much I tried, I couldn't explain with my mind what universal consciousness or "Infinite Intelligence," as Napoleon Hill called it, is. This is the essence of You. We are all connected to You, through You, and in You. We are You. We are the Infinite Intelligence manifested in the physical body that we call John, or Joan. So when John, or Joan, draws information from the universal consciousness, that is You feeding images to the mind of the body called John, or Joan.

2) One's subconscious mind – the memory. Our daily activity is stored in the memory. Everything we read, listen to, taste, feel, and smell is stored in the memory of our brain. As you know, some claim to have a good memory, while others claim to have a poor memory. The act of having a good memory is nothing but one's capacity to access this stored information, and as with any exercise, the more you practice, the better you get at it. Those who claim to have a bad memory don't **believe** they have been "gifted" with such a tool and simply don't even try to find that stored information; and if you are one

of these people who **believe** they have a bad memory, allow me to point out this: the act of **believing** that your memory is bad is the very cause of your lack of motivation to even try to access the stored information. With the few exceptions of brain damage in some individuals (and even that can be fixed), we all have stored memory in our brain for the information that we perceive through our five senses. An idea or a concept may be concluded from the information stored in the subconscious mind. The more education one has, the more information there is and the more complex the ideas are.

3) From the mind of another person who has just released the thought, or picture of the idea or concept, through conscious thought – every one of us has experienced, at least once, a situation in which we were thinking of a person and they called or wrote to us. We don't know yet whether the other person's thought of you reached your mind before the phone call, text, or email or if your thought of them impulsed them to get in touch with you, though I believe it works both ways. Recently, I was watching a documentary titled Superhuman, in which it was described and shown how one can be trained to see with the eyes of another, and they did this little experiment: a person sat in a room with a pen and paper thinking of the person who

left the room to visit a place unknown to them. While stimulating this "superhuman" side, the person in the room wrote down all that her body could feel and her mind was able to see. When she was taken to the place the other person had visited, she was shocked to realize that all of her notes matched the experience of this other person (Corey, 2020).

4) From another person's subconscious storehouse – similar to the previous source, whether it's from one's conscious thought or one's stored thought, the medium of transfer is the same. I told you earlier about my thought about the mobile phone; it turned out the mobile phone was actually in its early launch phase in the more developed countries, but my mind didn't know that because I was living in a communist country in which the TV was restricted to the communist party dogma, censored internal news, and limited entertainment.

You are the timeless link between all human minds throughout time: past, present, and future. It's the connection between ancestors and descendants. For You there is only one time – now! Everything happens now – ideas, actions, and thoughts; Everything is happening right now. If you're thinking, "Well, yeah, but yesterday I did this thing …" When you did that yesterday, you did it in the **now** – you were in the present; it's just the memory that recollects an action that you did in the now. You can't change that. It's like looking at an old picture or listening to an old recording. You remember with your mind the feelings that you had and you're having them once again, or crumbles of them, in the present. You're still living in the present moment, and in doing so we recreate the moment. Maybe that's the truth behind the classic saying that "history repeats itself" – we keep reliving the past in our minds and manifest it unconsciously.

> *"People like us, who believe in physics, know that the distinction between past, present and future is only a stubbornly persistent illusion. Time, in other words, is an illusion. The only reason for time is so that everything doesn't happen at once." —Albert Einstein*

> *"For the present is the point at which time touches eternity." —C. S. Lewis*

> *"Every second is of infinite value." —Johann Wolfgang von Goethe*

> *"Whether it's the best of times or the worst of times, it's the only time we've got." —Art Buchwald*

Eckhart Tolle, in his book *The Power of Now* says,

> Why does the mind habitually deny or resist the Now? Because it cannot function and remain in control without time, which is past and future, so it perceives the timeless Now as threatening. Time and mind are in fact inseparable.
>
> Imagine the earth devoid of human life, inhabited only by plants and animals. Would it still have a past and a future? Could we still speak of time in any meaningful way? The question "What time is it?" or "What's the date today?" – if anybody were there to ask it – would be quite meaningless. The oak tree or eagle would be bemused by such a question. "What time?" they would ask. "Well, of course, it's now. The time is now. What else is there?"
>
> Yes, we need the mind as well as time to function in this world, but there comes a point where they take over our lives, and this is where dysfunction, pain, and sorrow set in. (Tolle, 2000)

Time is the mind's way of recording thoughts and it needs time to organize them, not because it's necessary to the existence but to its memory. Time is bound to the existence of humanity on Earth. Any astronaut who went into space can confirm that time doesn't exist in outer space, or up and down; there is no east or west, light or heavy. These are all concepts of our mind to organize and orientate on Earth.

You, the universal consciousness, isn't bound by any of the mind's concepts, so if you want to draw information from Infinite Intelligence, mute your mind and its noise. Open the "superhuman" channel of communication and listen to You.

Miracles

What is a miracle? The miracle itself is the manifestation of You. When You manifests into the physical world, that is a miracle for the mind. We no longer call the ordinary things miracles because our mind is accustomed to them and they have become routine in our life. However, every insignificant thing that we see or do today was once a miracle. Take, for instance, fire; it's one thing that we all have in our lives and we take for granted: we cook, we warm up, and we build things. Fire was, at first, a "miracle sent by gods," but it was no longer that when our minds learned to understand and control it. The ability to control fire was a miracle, the new taste of food cooked with fire was a miracle, and lighting and heating a cave with fire was a miracle. When a new generation is born, that miracle becomes a norm of the world they've been born into, and the mind accepts it from the beginning as ordinary.

In other words, a miracle is an event inexplicable by the mind. Once the mind understands how it works, it loses its status of miracle. Throughout childhood our mind was blown away with miracles at every corner. Every new thing was another miracle for our mind. As we've grown and learned most of the things, we no longer consider them miracles, but something new of bigger proportions than our mind could comprehend would get the status of miracle until an explanation is given for it.

For the untrained mind, it's a miracle how a plane can lift off and travel through air without falling down, or how a steel ship can float without sinking. It was a miracle when the first disease was cured, and with every new disease that threatens the life of humans, a new miracle is born when healing is achieved. Every day I see stories on social media of miracles happening in people's lives.

Dr. Joe Dispenza (2020), in his book *You Are the Placebo*, tells about the miracle of his life. After being hit by a car while riding a bike, he was left paralyzed, and the doctors gave him no chance of ever walking. The mind immediately took that information, as coming from an authority, the doctors – his peers none the less, as a fact. Not many people have the power to refuse a diagnosis from their physician, but one of them was Dr. Joe Dispenza. He knew that You has power over the body and can make cells regenerate and heal the body. He knew that belief in his power to heal was the key to it. Every day, all day, for six weeks, he worked on changing the beliefs in his mind. Though, no signs of improvement showed up, he kept at it, and another four weeks later he managed to achieve, what the doctors called, a miracle. His body healed and he was able to walk home.

In 2020, according to World Health Organization, cancer took one life every three seconds, but these were only half of the people diagnosed with a form of cancer. The other half survived. That is a miracle happening every three seconds. I don't intend to take any credit from doctors, but I'm sure they can back me up on this when I say that the difference between life and death in a patient diagnosed with a life-threatening disease is in what happens in their mind – the belief they have in their ability to survive or not. Their belief keeps them fighting or not. If one's belief is that they're not strong enough to beat the disease, or that there is no reason for them to keep on fighting, well that surely is the end for their body. However, if one's belief is that they have a strong body that can overcome and defeat the disease, or that the doctors are only there to help them heal faster, or maybe they have someone at home they have to look after and can't afford to leave them on their own, well, these are the people who can heal from any disease.

The point I want to make is that an event is a miracle only in the eyes of those from outside who don't understand the process of achieving that particular thing. For the one involved in the process, who is focused on one thing only – the impossible and inexplicable thing for the mind – who can see themselves as if they have already achieved what they focus on, for them it isn't a miracle but a fact. They know they will achieve the "miracle" because in their mind they have already lived it. They can see themselves as already there and confidently can give thanks for the achievement.

If you listen to the story of any war veteran, the main thing that occupied their mind throughout the war was their thought of what they would do or what the world would look like after the war had ended. Their belief was in the life after the war. They may not have been able to predict what was happening from one moment to another or from one day to another, but they were sure that "When this thing is over, I will grow tomatoes in my back garden," or "I will ask her to marry me," or "I will take my kids to football." What their reason was is of little importance; the most important thing was the belief in their vision – that's how miracles are created.

More than 2000 years ago, a man known as Jesus, a carpenter by trade, and the son of God, according to more than thirty percent of the current world's population, discovered this secret and went on a quest to share it with the world. He explained that we have to believe before we receive or create. We have to give thanks for the things we want as if we have already received them, and to have faith in the outcome we desire as if it's our birthright. He went on to explain that we all had the same power he had because we are all the same; we all come from the same place, and we all have the same "father". Any of the miracles Jesus performed are available to you at the tip of your finger, but conditioned by one thing only – your belief in the realization of the thing you want.

Think about it! What did Da Vinci, Galileo, Newton, Morse, Edison, Marconi, Bell, and Tesla, to name a few, have in common? Their firm belief in the realization of the idea they had in their mind. They "knew" that no matter what the world may say, no matter if no one had ever done anything like it before, and no matter how impossible their idea may have seemed to their mind and the minds of others, their belief was so strong to the point they knew it to be true the same way you know right now that two and two is four. Their belief manifested in the form of knowledge, but not from their mind because, even before they started working on proving their idea, in their mind they had no clue how to bring their idea about. They used their mind to bring it about through trial and error, but they only spent their time on that idea because they believed it to be true.

Miracles, as explained above, have their cause in belief. If You believe in what the mind sees impossible, You can make miracles happen; anyone can make miracles happen. Listen to or read Rhonda Byrne's (2016) book *How The Secret Changed My Life* – it's filled with stories of miracles. People all over the world have shared how their life changed because they believed in something other than what society called the norm.

Chapter 7

THE POWER OF ACTION

"By thought, the thing you want is brought to you, by action, you receive it." (Wattles, 2014)

"Thoughts become things ®," says Mike Dooley. If you think of something, eventually it will become a thing. If you think of something for long enough, it will become a belief and that is a channel of manifestation. All the future thoughts that are in harmony with this channel manifest at a much faster rate. All the thoughts that aren't in harmony with the belief will have to go through a longer process.

So if one has a belief, like "Nobody ever loves me," all the thoughts in harmony with this belief manifest at a superfast rate, almost instantly, because the mind has already created the channel that flows toward that person with things that match their belief, and all they see around them is proof of that belief. If this person reads somewhere that everybody deserves to be loved, that's a new thought. Their belief and proof, so far, has only shown them the contrary, so even when the universe brings a person into their life who matches their thought and shows them love, because they're so overwhelmed by the amount of proof brought about by their belief, their mind may not even notice it.

The universe manifests all the thoughts that come through the mind, but what we see is determined by the filter of belief in our mind. Our beliefs aren't only channeling the manifestation process, but they're also the filter through which our mind observes the physical world. I was talking to a friend one day about a particular brand of cars, and he claimed he hadn't seen many of them around. A week after our conversation, we met again, and he pointed out that he had started to see this brand everywhere now. If a simple conversation can do this to our mind, imagine what a lifelong belief can do.

When you want to see different things in your life, know that your thoughts become things, and your beliefs channel the thoughts. If you want to change a belief, like "Nobody ever loves me," remember that this belief only brings about thoughts in harmony with it, so if you control your thoughts, and replace them with thoughts that you wish to manifest in your life, that old belief will start fading away and you will create a new channel for your new belief.

Most people, unaware of this process, get lost in the trial, and overwhelmed by their mind's arguments and proofs, they revert back to their original belief and carry on a "destined" life. These people are neither weak nor powerless; they're simply unaware that they have the power to control their own thoughts, and through this, their own life. All they see in their current circumstance has already been determined by yesterday's thoughts. They're unaware that a simple, consistent shift in their thoughts is all they need to turn their life around. Proof for this is the countless homeless people who became successful millionaires – read their stories!

Though, thought is all you need to manifest what you want to see in your life, to bring it about even quicker, another thing is required – action. I mentioned before of my thoughts about mobile phones and electric cars – they had been around for quite a while before I took action and purchased one.

So our thoughts do manifest, whether we take action on an idea that springs off that thought, or that thought is picked up by another human being on this planet and that person takes action and gives it form – it does manifest eventually. You could wait around a few years until someone brave enough picks up on your thought and makes your idea physically possible, or you could be the brave one and act on your idea.

I also mentioned my vision as a teenager about my future wife. If I hadn't taken action to go out and meet new people, it probably would've been a longer period of time between my thoughts and their manifestation. But I did take action; I did go out and I met her, and here we are twenty-one years later, still sharing a happy life.

When we are willing to change our life, we first have to change our thoughts, then we have to open our minds for new opportunities, and finally we have to act on those opportunities, because they do come and they come abundantly. Once you do that, a new channel of belief is created. Action is your power to create new belief channels. Acting on your new thoughts is creating new channels for manifestation.

I have heard a lot of times people saying, "I don't want my heart broken again," when talking about starting a new relationship. The truth is that it's not their heart that was broken; it's their mind's ego. You are pure energy, love, and life, and You can never be broken; You can never feel pain. That is all in our mind; that is your mind's attachment to that particular person – that is your mind's comfort zone. When You detach from your mind's ego and ignore all its noise, You can see that. There is no broken heart, there are no failures, and there's nothing to be afraid of, not even death. All of these are your mind's fears that have the role of protecting your body. Your mind is only programmed to keep you alive, not happy, not joyful, not in love, not elevated, and not successful – a simple basic breathing body.

To get anything you want, you must show your mind that you are determined to get it, you must train your mind to help you out, you must teach your mind to follow your lead, and you must take action, despite whether your mind knows there will be success or not. Once you've been through it, your mind will know it too, and its comfort zone would've expanded.

Our mind always assumes outcomes based on the limited information gathered in one life. If we don't experience, the mind doesn't learn, though the mind has the capacity to learn really fast. Take, for instance, a child whose mind hasn't built any barriers or walls to surround itself with; they will try everything and learn from every experience. We assume that's how humans are built – to learn faster when they're little. Then what? – we don't learn as fast? Is the memory filled up? No, we simply hold ourselves back from experiencing out of the fear of getting hurt, fear of failure, fear of being judged, or simply because we **believe** we are too old to make a difference.

If we stop exploring, our mind stops learning, and if we only act in the direction in which we know the outcome, we end up in a loop, living the same life over and over. There are people going on vacation in the same place every year, eating at the same restaurant, and ordering the same food because their mind is comfortable with the outcome. They know exactly what to expect from those places, they know exactly how their food will taste, and they even know if the restaurant has a new chef. How are these people different from a bird that migrates every year to the same place, a fish that swims in the same pond all their life, or a panda that only eats bamboo shoots? Their ability to imagine and create has been numbed by their mind through fears. It's created walls that protect the body like a prison protects the inmates, and as

Vernon Howard said, "You cannot escape a prison if you don't know you're in one." (AZ Quotes)

So the mind, for its comfort, will always aim to hold you within its walls "for your own protection." The longer You've been enclosed, the bigger the walls. Bob Proctor (n.d.), in his program *Thinking into Results*, called this the "terror barrier" – a barrier of the mind that releases all the fears at once into the body in an attempt to stop us from taking any action.

The mind only has knowledge of the past because that's where all the data it can use is stored. All that exists in the mind is the memory of the past events. Every time you want to try something new, there is a resistance within you, a fear of the unknown, or a fear of what could go wrong – that's the mind holding you back. Every time you go past your mind and trust "your gut," you discover something new, and the mind is sure to memorize that and expand on new experiences, but it only "judges" based on old experiences, memories, and events that happened in the past. When you resist change, it's actually your mind holding you back. When you allow yourself to change, it's You taking the lead.

Here you are, tired of your job, exhausted from too many hours of work, unable to sleep properly because there are so many things to be done at the office, and frustrated by not being able to spend more time with the family; You have no satisfaction, no motivation, and a desperate need for change. You're thinking of quitting your job and starting your own business. From the moment you even bring up such an idea, your mind will start throwing questions to shake it up: *Is this really what you want? Is this really a good idea? What if it doesn't work; what are you going to do then? Did you know that eighty-five percent of businesses fail within the first year?* and other random facts. The bravery in You wants to carry on, so you make a plan to break it to your family and to your boss. The mind now changes its tactic and releases emotional triggers: *But you've worked so hard. You've got so far. If you do this all your hard work will have been for nothing. How are you going to feed the family? They don't deserve to go through this. Your parents will be devastated if you do this.*

Most people give up on the idea at the first stage, and another good chunk of people will give up at the second stage, but the bravest ones will take action and do it anyway; they will stand up to their mind and show it that You are in control here, and You have the last say in all decisions, whether they've been bent by the mind or not. You didn't come to Earth to live in a box; You want to explore, relax, and experience all that this world has to offer.

Once that decision is acted on, the whole universe takes a huge turn to realign with your action. Through your action, you haven't only expressed a thought that you gave to the universe to produce when "the time's right," You have also forced the universe to take an abrupt turn, You've demanded the universe to give you a new layout for your life, and You've shown the universe you are serious about your thoughts and literally dug your own channel of manifestation.

The universe doesn't hesitate; it starts delivering on your new request right away, but your mind gets inundated with brand new information, and it starts to analyze, synthesize, and categorize all this information in an attempt to predict an outcome for which it still doesn't have enough information. It starts screaming, *I told you this was a bad idea. We're never going to get out of this alive. We have to get our old job back. This is never going to work because I have no idea how to do it and I've never done it before. Please go back to the old job, or at least let's get a similar job with a different company; it's going to be different, you'll see.*

You may feel overwhelmed by what your best friend, the mind, is bringing to the table, and there are the two options: you either go back to the comfort of the walls within which your best friend, your mind, held you safe and protected you from its rage or you shut it up. Accepting the change as part of the journey, and learning new things along the way, both from studying and experimenting, will eventually bring your mind along. It will discover new things and will get excited about the new things, and it will become once again eager to build up a new comfort zone. The universe helps a lot by making radical changes to support your decision, and it delivers all you need to make the transition as quick as possible so you can live on the new plane of existence that you've selected for yourself.

Some, including me, find it very useful, for this period of transition, to meditate; an exercise that helps You quiet your mind and connect with your "home" – the universe, the space of abundance and possibilities; it restores an old line of communication that was neglected for a long time because of your mind. You should never forget that You are an infinite being capable of things your mind can't imagine or comprehend, and You have the support of your entire family – the universe.

Once You detach yourself from the mind, and realize that You aren't your mind but its creator, You will have discovered your true power; peace and tranquility will flood your body, and new channels of manifestation will be being built.

Action is the key component of fast manifestation. When you think a thought, the universe brings it to life, not for the individual John or Joan but for You – the same You who resides in your body, John's body, and Joan's body. Through your action, that manifested thought is brought into the life experience of yourself; through John's or Joan's action, that manifested thought is brought into the life experience of John or Joan.

Say you're now looking for your ideal partner; you think of all the amazing features they will have, and you create a picture in your mind that is instantly released. The universe receives your mental picture and rearrange itself so that all the individuals who have those specific characteristics will cross your path – it brings them to you. When you meet them, you most probably aren't going to be able to recognize those features at first sight, so unless you take action, and ask them out for a drink so you can get to know each other better, you won't bring them into your life. There may be an instance where there is one individual who thought of a partner with some of your characteristics and they may be the one to take action and ask you out – accept it! It's still an action.

Now, let's say you want a particular bike, or car, or house. You build the picture in your mind, and the universe receives your request and rearranges itself for you to go past a store window that has that bike, or car, or takes you on a different route where you see the house. I remember when I came to the UK to work as a private hire (taxicab) driver; after a few months of hiring the car, I thought of buying my own car to use. Saving the money would've taken a lot of time, and the bank was out of the question as I had only been in the UK for a few months and I didn't even have a credit score at that time. One day, as I was waiting for my next fare, another driver from the same company parked his car next to mine. From one conversation to another, he asked me why I didn't have my own car. After I explained my reasons, he offered to lend me the money and he even found the car for me – all I had to do was to accept his offer. Through thought the universe brought this person to me, and through action I achieved my vision of owning a car.

If your mental picture doesn't have an equivalent in the physical world, the universe will put that picture into the minds of the bike or car designers, or the minds of the architects, and that picture of yours will be created. When you cross paths with the manifestation of your mental image, you only need to take action and take it. And I don't mean to take it from another without paying the price of their asking, because that creation is the work of another You who received your mental picture and acted on your idea to give it a physical form. For their efforts they deserve that price; the same as you deserve the price you're asking for your services.

"Yeah, but that house costs so much that I may need five lives to get the money to pay for it," some may say. That isn't You; that is the limited mind that can only see one way of making money – the way that individual has experienced. A janitor's mind may think they can only get money from cleaning, a teacher's mind may think the only way to get money is from the school where they teach, and a mechanic's mind may think their only way to make money is by fixing cars – remember that the Wright brothers were bike mechanics. A janitor could build a successful cleaning business, a teacher may be able to create online programs, and the mechanic can become an engineer.

If you search the internet for successful people, you'll discover hundreds of them who started as cleaners or living on the streets. That wasn't their limitation. Every successful individual had one dream and the courage to go for it. If you need more money, you will find a way to make more money. Simply ignore the limitations of the mind and challenge it to seek ways through which to achieve your dreams, and when you find the way, just act! Believe in your ability to bring about with your thoughts any solution you may need for all the problems your mind may point out.

Risk – what is it, and how to eliminate it?

Our mind gets quickly attached to things and doesn't detach easily from them. It clings on to all the things that it gets comfortable with, and it sticks to them because they're part of its comfort zone. When I bought my first car, I loved it so much; I used to clean it every day, and drive it every day – it was my pride. It wasn't a new car, and it wasn't a special car that I dreamed about – it was simply my first car. Then, things started breaking in it, parts needed to be replaced, money was spent, and stress was involved – all because I was so attached to it. The moment I decided to scrap it, my mind started screaming. Losing something our mind is attached to may be painful, but through this process I allowed the law of vacuum to manifest; I created a void to be filled with something else that suited my new state of being.

Every day we learn new things, and every day we grow, but the attachment to old and comfort keeps us in the same place; it holds us back like the parking brake in a car, or the anchor of a boat. We can't move freely and advance in life because of our attachments. We can't find happiness in marriage because our mind is too attached to our partner and is too afraid to lose them. We can't find happiness in our job because our mind is too attached to it and is afraid to lose it. Our mind can't let us take the necessary action toward the achievement of happiness because of the fear of losing what it's attached to, and that's how the expression "A bird in the hand is worth two in the bush" came to be born in the mind.

The truth is, the most valuable things in life aren't those that are the most expensive but those that are free. Life is free and is more valuable than the most expensive boat. Love is free and is more valuable than the most expensive car. A hug is free and is more valuable than the most expensive watch. Our mind puts value on the physical because it can't perceive the invisible, so we go on shopping sprees in the hope we'll fill some voids that could be simply filled with a human touch. If you were to take the money that you'd have spent on an expensive dress, shoes, watch, car, or whatever it is that your mind may think would make you feel better, and give it to a homeless person, a charity, or do anything else that would touch another human's life, you'd feel much better.

Everything you'll ever need is already within You. All the material things are simply there to help

You experience the physical world. It's one experience to drive an old rusty car, and it's another experience to drive a brand-new shiny one. All creations exists for us to experience the physical world. We don't need things to be happy; we yearn for the experience. We get into a relationship because we want to feel love; though the misconception is that love has to be received in order to be felt, in reality, love is to be given, and in exchange for it we receive what we yearn for. We jump out of planes and go bungee jumping to feel the thrill. We eat delicious foods so we can feel the taste, we create music, paintings, and sculptures so we can share a feeling. We travel so we can enjoy new experiences. Things are just so we can experience the physical world.

So when we take action to move up in life, in search of a new experience, we don't risk anything; we merely make room for something bigger and better that is in harmony with our new state of mind – something that will lead us to experience something new. The mind, on the other hand, doesn't see it that way. The mind is possessive. The mind doesn't like sharing. The mind doesn't like change. It's only after the change, when all is settled and fear is gone, that the mind gets comfortable again. Once we do a thing a few times, the mind gets comfortable with that change.

I mentioned my first car and my mind's addiction to it. After that, every two or three years I changed cars – different brands, sizes, models, etc. My mind can't wait for the new car and the thoughts that come from my mind changed from we can't afford another car to we can't afford not to get another car, and all the arguments that happen inside my mind now are for the action – the pro action. My mind has shifted from a "comfortable with what we have" setting to a "looking forward to the new adventure" setting.

When we take action despite the circumstances, and despite what the programmed mind has to say about it, we expand the knowledge of the mind, we reprogram the mind to "see" things differently, and we build new habits, new channels, of manifestation that bring about more opportunities for our mind to see and take action.

Let's go back to the physical things our mind clings to. When one's life on this earth ends, the amount of riches gathered equals nothing for the one who gave his last breath because they're physical riches that can only be used in a physical world, and for the physical body to experience. You, as a spiritual being, have other values, and these values don't have an equivalent in the physical world other than that of experience. How much does your happiness cost? How much does your relationship with your partner, your children, your parents, or your siblings cost? Aren't these priceless and timeless? No amount of money or presents can pay for these.

So what are You attached to? What is holding You back? What do You risk? There is nothing in the physical world that can amount to something worthy of Your attachment. Money can be made again – the second time is usually quicker and in higher quantities. Houses can be rebuilt – the second time usually more beautiful and cozier, and so on. The relationships with your spouse, children, parents, and siblings have nothing to do with the amount of riches you have gathered so far, and if they appreciate that more than they appreciate you, it means that you have sent the wrong signal to them; you led them to believe that you are those things and lost yourself in them and identified yourself with them, and it's probably the right time to amend your priorities. Always look at things as if they're disposable tools that are there to help you live a fulfilled life. And always look at people as if they're infinite beings! When you look at it like this … Do you still see risk? Do you still feel attached to things?

Many people claim that their riches are gathered so they can leave them to their beloved children. Remember one thing: those are yours – your work, your likes, and your experiences. Your children have already experienced them, so if you want your children to relive the same life as you over and over after you're gone, and if you want your children to have no personality of their own but the one you want for them (because you've lived already and know what's best for them), then you will allow your mind to satisfy its selfish thirst and attempt to replicate your life in the minds of your children.

Whatever you created and built in your life was for your own desires and experiences. Every individual is unique and has unique desires. I often hear parents saying to their children, "I thought you wanted to do this," or "I thought you liked that" – in reality, it was a wish in the parents' minds, who thought they could nurture their children to desire the things they never had the courage to pursue. In their regret for not acting on their dream, they hope that their children could satisfy that thirst and they can eventually experience whatever it is they unconsciously trained their children to pursue.

I love my father from the bottom of my heart because he always wanted what was best for us as children. He wanted for us to live a more fulfilled life than he did, and not because he didn't have the courage to pursue his dreams but because he didn't have bigger dreams for himself. So he nurtured me to pursue something he thought would offer me a life of comfort and happiness. Though that wasn't my wish, I tried it so I wouldn't upset him because I love him very much. Eventually, I couldn't do it anymore and gathered the courage to tell him – his mind was shocked.

The point I want to make is that, even if you love your children and you want what's best for them, and you work hard all your life to facilitate an easier one for them, it may not be what their deepest desire is – it is your desire. If you want to leave them something after you're no longer physically on this earth, leave them something no thief can take, no water can flood, and no fire can burn – leave them knowledge, and cherish all the moments you can with them. Instead of buying them more and more expensive toys, the value of which they have no capacity to appreciate anyway, you could spend an extra hour per day with them. And don't say, "I've got work to do, and I don't have time" – how you fill your time is a choice. Too many people advance in life to realize they forgot something along the way – they forgot to spend time with those who are most important to them, for whom, allegedly, they worked so hard all their life. When we realize that a relationship is much more valuable than any physical fortune, our perception of risk will shift.

Everything that exists in the physical plane is subjected to time – our life, our friends, family, material possessions, etc. – and even though everything is constantly changing, our mind attaches itself to the things and people that become part of its comfort zone. The whole physical universe is constantly transforming. From the cells in our body that multiply and die so we can grow and transform, to the acorn that falls to the ground and grows into an oak tree, to the moon that revolves around the earth, to the sun and stars, and galaxies – everything is changing and transforming. The only constant is the energy that makes them live and transforms them – You.

The world exists because of You and for You. In a manner of speaking, uneasy for the mind to comprehend, all the things and all the people in our life exist because of You: parents, children, friends, house(s), car(s), job(s), etc. are all physical projections of your thoughts, and they're creations of imagination. Everything that exists right now in your life is a result of your thoughts – if you have enough of these riches, your mind may be proud to hear this, though if you don't have them, your mind may hate me reading this, but all of it is the manifestation of your past thoughts.

Once you wrap your head around this concept and understand that You can create anything you want and You can bring about as many people as you need to experience the life You wish for yourself, you'll realize that nothing is ever lost. Everything that comes into your life has a purpose to serve and once you've experienced that something a thing was created for and it no longer serves a purpose, it falls behind to make room for other things to be created and help You experience something else.

The mind, bound by its existence to this physical plane, attaches to physical things and clings on to them so it can identify itself with them, and so it can identify with the achievements and possessions. Have you noticed that when one talks about their life, they say **my** spouse, **my** children, **my** house, **my** car, and **my** money, as if they own them, and when one or all of these are lost, they grieve? The grievance is but a rupture from an attachment. Now, this may sound cold and insensible to some readers who have lost a spouse, parents, or children to hear that their dearest served their purpose and that's why they're gone, but please bear with me just a little bit longer.

Imagine that you, your family, and friends have decided to play a virtual game, and in this game, each one of you plays a character. The game is designed in such a way that each character has a role to play that leads to the completion of the game. Along the way, some characters step forward to do what they do best, while other characters hold back waiting for their turn based on their achievements and abilities in the game. Some characters may step into something, or fall off something, and that's the end of it. The rest carry on with the mission of the game, while the one who lost their character goes into the kitchen to bring some popcorn and drinks for everybody else. At the end of the game you all are having a good laugh and have a good memory to remember until next week's game.

While playing that game, did the characters know they were characters, or was it you who knew they were characters? Would you still suffer the loss of a character knowing it was just a character and next time you could start over and choose a different character?

Once You no longer identify with the mind – your character – there will be no more suffering or loss because You know that nothing is actually lost. For the mind to understand this is hurtful because the mind only lives this one life, while You get to live as many lives as You want and play whatever characters You want. If you've lost someone, simply imagine they're in the kitchen bringing popcorn and drinks and that once this game is over, you can get together and watch a movie, go for a walk, or do whatever fun things You want.

Another reason for suffering is that we resist change. Everything changes in nature, and in the world – it's a natural process. The seed in the ground changes into a plant, the day changes into night and vice versa, the clouds change into rain, and a child changes into an adult – we change every time we change environment. However, when we resist change, when we want to keep the things the same way, or when we want to be the same as we used to be yesterday, or yesteryear, that's when we start suffering because everything around us changes and we no longer fit in there.

In order to fit in the new environment, in the new times, and in order to absorb and experiment the new sensations, we must adapt, and we must allow ourselves to go with the flow. The action we must take is actually none; we only have to allow ourselves to adapt and to accept the change. The action of resisting change is what makes us suffer because it feels like it's "me against everyone else," and the mind tries to find other similar people with whom to make a common ground to resist change; to fight against the attitude of the new generation, fight against new government, fight against new ways, and remember "the good old days."

You are an unlimited being. You live beyond mind and body. You are the life of the mind and body. You are beyond the physical world, and as your creation, the physical world only exists because of You. Everything has been created for You so You can experience it. It doesn't matter where you were born, the color of your eyes or skin, the height or weight of your body, or your gender or sexual interest. All that matters is that at any point You can change your environment with your thoughts. If you don't like something, You can change it.

It's needless to say that the world around You is your creation, and also the other people in it, and though you can change your world, you can't change the people – the other You. The same as you, they create their own world. You exist in their life because of their thoughts, they exist in your life because of your own thoughts, and the universe made possible your worlds' interconnection. If at any point, they change their thoughts and their new world doesn't include you, that is when the separation is produced, and there is nothing you can do to change that. It's their experience and you should respect that.

To summarize this chapter, nothing is ever yours. You don't possess anything and yet You create it all. The mind's limited perception of this concept only holds us back from experiencing more in this life by clinging on to material things. Everything is meant to change to match the new thoughts and states of vibration. Everything has a purpose that matches your thoughts. When your thoughts change, everything changes. When you take action, you act on new thoughts and ideas, which change the course of the world as you know it. Action is the fastest way to having new experiences. Nothing is ever lost – they've just served their purpose, and you risk losing nothing because you're creating something else. It's like erecting scaffolding to build a house – your house is finished, but you're so attached to the scaffolding that you find it hard to take it down. Once you let go of the scaffolding, the beauty of the house is revealed.

Whatever ideas you may have, you'll never know what they look like until you act on them and bring them into the physical world. If you don't do it, someone else will, because if you had that idea, so has everyone else, and it's just a matter of time before it will come to life. Fear of losing comes from the mind and its attachment to things. You're not risking anything when acting on something new, and whatever you think you may lose, you can always create it back with a simple thought, which will pop up in your life even faster because you already have the manifestation channel. But you didn't need me to tell you all this because You already knew that – I only reminded you.

Chapter 8

HABITS

The most useful tool of the mind – habits – are little programs that run in the background, and most of the time, we're not even aware of them, unless we are questioned about them or we take a moment to analyze them.

Think about it! When you ride a bike for the first time, you have to pay attention to every detail and focus on balance, brakes, pedals, etc. – it's kind of exhausting, isn't it? Imagine you had to do this kind of thinking all the time, to put in all this effort every time you rode a bike … It's not as enjoyable now, is it? But because we have this amazing tool that learns and repeats, we get to enjoy a bike ride stress free. Now think about other things you do by default, like dressing, walking, writing, driving, typing, etc. – they're all little programs that run in our mind for us so we can focus on enjoying life.

But programs are just that. They're not personal. However, the outcome of the habit may be the one that changes your life and your life's perspective. Let's talk about smokers. Smoking is a habit that people are doing unconsciously. They buy cigarettes by default, they light them up by default, and so on. Even in tough times, when they're short on money and have to cut expenses on something, they're not thinking of quitting smoking; they're looking into buying cheaper ones or cheaper alternatives that will keep that habit running. What started as "just a cigarette" next to a drink with friends becomes a habit that takes over one's life.

I chose this habit as I got to live with it for a while and I talk from experience. If you allow your mind to control your life, in these situations you have no say in it. Your mind doesn't know whether smoking is a good thing or not. For your mind this is just another program that "must" run because that's what it's there for. So what do You do when You realize it has taken over Your life, is draining your savings, and destroying your health? You change the programming and direct it toward something else or simply shut it down completely.

"Easy for you to say," I have heard so many times. Easy to say and easy to do. When you hear in your head all the reasons why you're different from me and you can't do what I do because you've got the life that you have – that's not You! That's your mind protecting its integrity – its Ego. Your mind knows it's doing a good job because it only does what it has been programmed to do, so it won't let that go easily.

And I agree; you can't simply quit because someone tells you that You can or because you read it in a book. But you can surely do so when You realize that You are the master, not the mind, and You decide what it's going to be. When You take the decision to stop whatever habit your mind has created, that becomes a law – the new rule – and the program stops. I was smoking about forty cigarettes daily at one point, and one day I realized I'd have to choose between smoking for another day or eating for another week. Then and there I realized I had the power to change that and I took the decision to stop smoking, and I did.

That was so much easier than I've been led to believe. People around me kept telling me that you can't simply stop smoking: "You have to downgrade – to reduce the numbers until you stop" and "It doesn't happen overnight; it takes time." I lost a lot of friends because I proved them wrong.

What I realized out of this was: 1) I'm stronger than what others think I am, which gave me a boost of confidence, 2) People always talk from their own point of view, 3) They aren't friends after all if you lose them that easily, and 4) I can do anything I put my mind to.

It may not be easy to understand why our mind works the way it does, or why it has been built this way, but the most amazing thing is understanding **how** it works so we can use it to our advantage. When people discovered that plants grow out of seeds, they became farmers. When Romans discovered that water flows from elevated planes toward the ocean, they built aqueducts and brought water into the cities. The Wright brothers used Newton's discovery, the law of gravitation, to lift planes into the air. After Hertz proved the existence of the electromagnetic waves predicted by Maxwell, Marconi built his own wave-generating device, which today we know as the radio.

Today we have water running through all the cities in the world, we can fly anywhere on the globe, and we can send messages and speak with people in space because, as humans, we've used the discoveries to our advantage, so why not use the information we know about habits to our benefit also?

First of all, understanding how habits are created is the most important part. In simple terms, an action repeated a number of times becomes a habit. For an advanced study, I recommend James Clear's (2018) book: *Atomic Habits*. Now that we know how habits are created, we can make our own tailored habits, and we can also eliminate the useless and harmful ones.

So if you want to be a successful person, create good habits. Train your mind to read and study every day, give a percentage of your earnings to charity on a consistent basis, and transfer a percentage of the money you earn into a savings account on every payday – these are habits that help you live a successful life. If you want to live a happy life, make a habit of telling your spouse/partner how amazing they are and let them know that you appreciate everything they do. If you want to live a healthy life, make a habit of going for a run every morning, or a long walk every evening; make a habit of buying healthy foods and eating at regular intervals, or whatever you believe will help. Whatever it is you want to achieve, there are one or more habits that you can create in your life that can help you achieve your goal.

On the other hand, if there are habits that no longer serve you but you're still doing them, you can simply get rid of them – I know that some readers will lose it when they hear the word "simply" because they "know" it's not that simple. "Know" is another word to describe belief. I know that I can walk means I believe that I can walk. I know that I can do that means I believe that I can do that. Though some people think "believe" is somehow weaker than "know" because "know" is a result of proven facts and "believe" involves variables, the truth is that they're one and the same. The only difference is in whether the action has a backup result or not.

So if you wished to do something and **believed** you could, you tried and succeeded, and now you **know** you can. If you wished to do something but you **believed** you couldn't, you've quit before you succeeded, and now you **know** you can't. People often allow their peers to decide for them whether they may be capable or not, though they always talk from a personal point of view. When someone says, "You can't do that," what they're actually saying is, "I can't do that, so don't do it because you'll hurt my ego if you succeed."

You already know that a habit is the result of an action you repeated for a while. Maybe at that point it was a coping mechanism that helped you get past certain things. For instance, smoking is associated with calming down, or calming your nerves. Coming out of an intense meeting, a cigarette could have been something that helped the body release tension. After a while it became a habit to smoke after every meeting, and then at every break. Smoking is also associated with socializing – you go out with your friends, you're having fun, and they draw out a cigarette and so do you. After a while, even though you're no longer going out with the same friends, the habit is still associated with going out and here we go …

When you realize that a habit is just that – a habit of the mind – and you aren't defined by your habit because You aren't your mind, your point of view changes. You're no longer experiencing the event as a player but as a coach, you observe from a distance, analyze and decide if what the player is doing will help them win, and you can coach your player to their next move. The player knows the coach is there to help them win and executes the moves given.

If you want to learn to write in Chinese, Japanese, Korean, Greek, or any language that you currently don't know and is completely different from the language in which you habitually write, your consciousness – You – directs your hands, like a coach directs their player, to print every character on paper. After a while your hand, the player, learns to do the characters without your conscious involvement. The same applies with unlearning a habit.

Firstly, You decide to quit smoking, stop drinking, reduce food intake, remove unhealthy food from your diet, or whatever habit you want to stop. Decision is the key to it all. "I'll try" won't do the trick. When you say, "I'll try," you don't even believe you can, and if you don't believe, you won't. When You decide to achieve something, there is no stopping You – no matter how many times you fall, or how many times you fail, You will keep getting up and keep trying until you succeed. Decide that you will, no matter what. Yeah, but ... That's only the mind talking and You aren't your mind. Your mind may try to hold you back in its comfort zone because that's all it knows, though once you understand You aren't your mind, you will understand that you aren't its limitations either, and through your experience – through your will to go beyond your mind's limitations – you'll only show your mind there is more to it than what it knows. Through this exercise you help your mind expand its comfort zone; therefore, making it easier for You to explore even further.

There's always going to be the trigger: the meeting, the lunch break, or going out, but You will be there too, and when the trigger urges your mind to kick in the habitual sequence, You remind your player that this is a move you're no longer playing, and the player listens and holds back. The moment you slip into identifying with your mind again, you step on the field – you're no longer the coach; you are a player. So when that happens, simply step off the field.

After a while, you won't only get rid of a habit, you also teach your mind the master habit – listening to You. Once you have achieved this habit, there is no stopping you from expanding, exploring, learning, being, or having anything you want. The moment You master your mind is the moment You master Your Own Universe.

Chapter 9

RELATIONSHIPS

Whether we're talking about a relationship with your parents, siblings, spouse, partner, children, relatives, friends, acquaintances, co-workers, or simply people you meet for the first time, there is always going to be two of you in that relationship. What we call a relationship is the string that connects two people, and this string can have any form, size, color, shape, and strength.

I spoke in the previous chapters about the unlimited power You have and the ability of your mind to manifest anything you think. You aren't alone! You aren't the only one who has unlimited power and a mind with the ability to manifest any thought. There are billions of You on this planet.

Everywhere you look there is another You moving around in a body and living in a world created by their own mind that happens to intersect with yours, and not by chance but by design – Your design.

Every person in your life, and every person you meet, is a direct response of the universe to your own thoughts. You haven't created the people; you demanded the universe to intersect them with your life through your thoughts. Your mind may not know what these people's role in your life is, but the universe sent you the perfect match for your thoughts. In other words, there is a connection between You and every single person that crosses your path.

Every single person is a helping hand who comes to support your thoughts. Whether sometimes we think they're "sent by God" to save us or they're just a nuisance, an "idiot in traffic" or "annoying colleague," they're each and every one of them attracted to our own lives by our very own thoughts. I know this is a big chunk to swallow, but look on the bright side; when you see something in people that you don't like, you won't have to discipline them, and you won't have to shout out of your car's window or sound your horn – all you have to do is change your thoughts, and these people or their actions will be replaced by other people and actions that will match your new thoughts.

Do you know why we blame others for unfortunate events? Because from our mind's perspective we did all that we could do with the knowledge we had, accurate and possible, to the best of our ability. From the mind's limited capacity, there was nothing more to be done because we only have in our mind what we have experienced in our life, so when anything goes wrong, it can't be our minds' fault, but that's just the mind's opinion, and remember – **You are not your mind!** So when someone blames you for their unhappiness or "bad luck," remember that you are but a witness to their thoughts and shouldn't take it personally. The same applies when you feel like blaming others – they're just witnesses to your creative thoughts.

"There is a legendary story of a man knowns [sic] as Dr. Ihaleakala Hew Len, who cured every patient in the criminally insane ward of a Hawaii'i State Hospital – without ever seeing a single patient." (Radhe, n.d.). Dr. Len was a master teacher of the ancient Hawaiian practice of Ho'oponopono. He learned that we are 100% responsible for everything and everyone who comes into our lives. In his case, he also included these criminally insane patients.

"Dr. Len set up an office within the hospital to review his patients' files," but not the patients. "While he looked at their files, he would work on himself," (Radhe, n.d.) and by using this potent forgiveness and releasing practice, he was able to clear his mind of subconscious blocks, unconsciously accepted beliefs, thoughts, and memories that he didn't even know he had.

> The legendary Hawaiian healing and cleansing method Ho'oponopono [...] is based on healing through loving oneself. Dr. Len repeated the words "I love you" and "I am sorry" over and over again while reviewing each file individually. After a few months, the patients who were shackled were allowed to walk freely, [...] [some] were taken off medications, and even the hopeless cases were [...] released back into society (Radhe, n.d.).

So over a period of four years, all the patients were healed. In addition, even the staff who had been calling in sick all the time, or had quit, had now returned and "loved coming to work."

The same as Dr. Len, you too have the power to fix your own environment – in line with your own thoughts. Dr. Len studied these kinds of patients long before he got to work in that ward. While studying them, he created thoughts in his mind, which manifested accordingly. Now, being in this new environment created by his own thoughts, aware of the power of manifestation, and taking 100% responsibility for the people he attracted into his life, he took it upon himself to help them by healing and cleansing himself. He could have chosen simply to quit the job, change his thoughts, and rearrange his life in a different way; however, he also realized that if he didn't do it, all those subconscious blocks of his mind, and unconsciously accepted beliefs, would've stayed with him and sprang out whenever triggered.

When we take responsibility for our world, which includes the people who we meet, we are in control. If we reject the idea that we attracted these people, we are no longer in control, we can no longer control the environment from within, and we assume that everything outside of us is chaos and simply happens to us because of some sort of vengeful gods who want to punish us for whatever thing our mind brings up to the surface.

You are in control of your life. You are in control of the events that happen in your life. You are in control of the people who are attracted into your life, and you are in control of choosing to accept them or not. Though some people may think, "Yeah, but I didn't choose my parents and siblings" – that may be true, or you may be a manifestation of their thoughts – but people also didn't choose the color of their skin or their eyes, didn't choose to be born on one continent or another, or in a peaceful country or war zone. For our mind, none of these seem to have been chosen, but until we find the real answer to these questions, which most probably will happen after we leave the body altogether, the next best thing is to accept it as it is. Whether you believe in reincarnation and this life is a manifestation of your past life's thoughts, or you believe this life is a game and this time around you chose this environment, or whatever story You want to tell your mind, simply accept it as it is, and accept the people in your life for what they are. If you don't like them, remember that it's hard work to change them and there are no guarantees you'll be able to do that without triggering some other events you won't like, and it's much easier to control your own thoughts without interfering with their freedom of choice, and without triggering unwanted events and circumstances in your life.

All the people we meet are there to show us something that we created with our thoughts. Respect and love them for they are only messengers – the universe's response to your thoughts. We can't change the people in our life, but we can surely change the way we communicate with them. By changing our own thoughts – despite the reality our mind sees – we change the way people act toward us. Neville Goddard (2015), in his book Feeling Is the Secret, told a story about a designer who came to him because she had big problems with her boss. After listening to her problems, he asked her if she creates scenarios in her mind about their conversations. She admitted that, on her way to work, she'd imagine him disliking her work and how she'd tell him everything that she couldn't tell him in person. Goddard explained to her this principle of manifestation and how she had created this situation with her thoughts and asked her to change the story she was telling herself. She acted right away, and within a very short period of time, her boss completely changed his attitude toward her.

If you feel like your parents don't treat you in a certain way – that is the direct result of your own thoughts. You are the one who thinks that way about yourself, and through these thoughts and through your body's vibration, you are demanding the universe to make them treat you the same way. Change your thoughts! However you want them to act toward you, create the picture in your mind of what you want, and become in your imagination the person that you want them to see. Use the technique Dr. Len used to cleanse your mind from unwanted thoughts, and unconsciously accepted beliefs deeply embedded in your mind that you may not even be aware of, and use Goddard's idea to change the story that you play on the screen of your mind.

If you feel like your children don't treat you in a certain way, change your thoughts, and change the image of yourself. Children are, generally, a reflection of the image of their parents. When they're born, their mind is empty of experiences and memories. The people from whom they learn first and most are the closest ones – parents and siblings. These are the people who determine their truth and influence their reality. You can tell a child that the sun is blue and the grass is red, and they will live for a while believing that – until their belief is challenged by the rest of the world. If you want your child to change their way, show them the "right" way – be the person you want them to be, and to do so, you have to think you are what you want them to be. Between what you do and what you say, they will always pick what you do and what your body vibrates in harmony with. If what you say is in harmony with what you do and believe to be "right," they will listen to you also.

When it comes to your life partner, if you apply the principle described in this book that You are a limitless, infinite being living in a human body and you are both choosing to be with each other, the connection between you should be nothing but harmonious. On the other hand, all discrepancies, suffering, stress, unhappiness, and unfaithfulness come from the mind's need for authenticity, acceptance, and justice. It isn't You who wants to be loved; it's your mind – You wants to give love. It isn't You who feels betrayed when your partner engages in a physical (or emotional) relationship with another human being; it's the ego of your mind. You wants your partner to be happy no matter what, with or without you in their life.

You are a pool of love, self-reliant, and in no need of attachment and dependency of another human being, though You choose so. If all you do is to selflessly give your love to your partner with no expectancy of an exchange, you have achieved the highest form of love. If you hear a voice in your head that says, "Yeah, but that's not fair, as it should come both ways," or "How long before I can see a response?" or any other similar things, know that it isn't You pointing out these questions but your mind.

A "soulmate" can be any soul on this planet as long as you look at the soul and not the manifestation of the body which it inhabits. You and I are the same and One. There is no difference; no comparison. Only the mind – in its egoistic state – feels the need to be compared and to compare, to measure and to be loved. From its materialistic source, it feels the need to possess both things and people.

When we choose a partner, the mind automatically assigns "mine" to them: my partner, my love, my husband, or my wife. This, therefore, leads to the feeling of jealousy and betrayal when we imagine that "my" partner may be involved with someone else. Emphasis on imagine – the mind, out of fear of losing the one it's attached to, brings up on its screen possible scenarios, which in turn create more fear in the body. The You within doesn't feel attachment and doesn't need assurance. The You within is pure love, and love is so abundant that there is no need to ask for it – just give; love is for giving.

When we feel a lack of love, we think from our mind's perspective. The mind can't create love; You are the source of love and you can never drain it from another. Love can only be given, and only given love can fill holes in another. Say, for instance, you are in a relationship and your partner is "cold." You can't ask them to show you love. The moment you do that you expose your mind's need. Your mind is the one seeking love from your partner. What you can do instead is look within You; start loving yourself and make your mind find comfort in being loved, overflow your own body with love, and then direct the overflowing love toward your partner. This way you're filling the emptiness in your mind, and allowing it to detach from the need of being loved by your partner; Allowing them to really have a choice and to feel that they aren't possessed but loved and cared for – that's what will make them love you.

Sometimes it only takes a gesture, like a hug or a kiss, to see them radiating love, while other times it takes more than that, but rest assured that the more love and freedom you give them, the closer you are to making them happy and free, and that is what will make them feel attracted to you. And if you keep going, there is guaranteed success that they will be able to "show" you their love eventually.

If you're not in a relationship right now, but you do want that perfect relationship with the perfect partner, know this: what you see with your physical eyes is only a fraction of what you can see with Your eyes. Your physical eyes can only see 120° at one time and no further than three miles, while Your eyes can see 360° and as far as you can imagine both in distance and time. A "pretty face" doesn't make a perfect partner but a trophy. A pretty face is something that you show off to your friends.

When it's just the two of you, the pretty face doesn't outweigh the things you struggle to accept in your partner, and conflicts are very likely to appear. I'm pretty sure you've seen "perfect looking" couples in the media that – after a while – break up, fight in public, etc. A pretty face will also be the first reason for jealousy. But don't get me wrong, please; I'm not suggesting you shouldn't engage in a relationship with someone whose looks please the physical eyes. What I'm saying is that once you look at someone with Your eyes and see that perfect, beautiful soul, and start appreciating that instead, the beauty of that soul will start manifesting through their body anyway.

If you are with anyone, love them from the bottom of Your heart and help them shine as bright as they can, and you will witness the most amazing physical transformation that no surgical doctor can ever achieve!

But you can make it easier by finding a partner who matches your desire. To start with, create an image of the type of partner you want – just before you go to sleep, bring up on the screen of your imagination all you want to see in your partner: how they look at you, how they talk to you, the joy they bring into your life, and so on, and think of them as you drift away in sleep.

Try not to put a face on that person if you want a fast manifestation, though if you want a particular person who you like very much, it means you already know who you want, and all you need to do is ask them out to learn more about them. You can have as a partner any person on this planet if you choose to do so; however, for you two to have a long and harmonious relationship, there is a need for both parties to accept and want to pursue it. You can find ways to get together with whomever you want, and you will, if your desire is strong enough and your determination unbeatable, but that won't guarantee your happiness! That will only guarantee an achieved goal.

If they say yes, you get to discover more and more about them, and choose to accept them for who they are or not. If they say no, it means they have their eyes on someone else or they don't see themselves in a relationship with you, so let it be. It's your mind that gets attached to people, not You. It's your mind that needs that particular person, not You.

The truth is, if they have the courage to say no, you are in luck because you then know to move on; it's no different from what it was before you asked. You weren't in a relationship with them before you asked, and you aren't in a relationship after they said no either. Though, if they said yes, you may be one step closer to a beautiful relationship. Bear in mind one thing – they're free spirits as well; free to love whom they choose, and free to change their mind if they choose to do so. Don't ask of them what you wouldn't want them to ask of yourself, and even so, respect their liberty and freedom. You should never expect them to act in a certain way either; just accept them for who they are and love them for what they are. If you can't do that but insist on carrying on with that relationship, you'll end up in a nightmare relationship in which both of you will suffer. So if, after you meet them, you discover they don't have a personality that you like very much, remember that physical appearances don't make up for the attitude of a person, and you can attract to you the right person who ticks all the boxes. Don't settle for less than you deserve.

Once you've created the image of the person you want, you can forget about it; there is no need to dwell upon it because your message has been received, so just be You. Be kind, joyful, and loving with every single soul you meet on a daily basis. You don't have to search for your partner because that partner will be attracted into your life by the power of your thoughts and actions, and by the power of their thoughts and actions. The two of you will be the answer to each other's thoughts and vibration – you will be each other's perfect match.

The secret to a perfect relationship is to accept there is no limitation. If they want to leave, let them go, or if they want to be with someone else, let them find their own happiness. The only thing that should concern you is to do your part and love them as much as you can and not judge their actions and choices. As long as you've done your part, the rest will fall to place, and if in the end, you're not going to end up together after all, that's for the better! But it's their choice to leave or to stay; it's not your job to hold them close to you. And more often than you think, even if you treated them with respect and love, they may still leave because they may not be on the same vibrational level with you. But eventually they will realize what they left behind and it'll be down to them, once again, to choose to return, and down to you to choose to accept them back into your life.

If you are being You, and show love, respect, and kindness to all those you meet on a daily basis, the one you seek – the one who matches your vibration – will see this and they will be attracted to these attributes of yours and they will love you for who you are, and not for how you look; they will want to be with you and you won't have to ask them to stay. Become what you want to attract. Be the person you want to spend the rest of your earthly life with, or part of it.

Above all, in any relationship, guide your attitude by this one universal law that binds us all to each other, also known as the Golden Rule – do to others what you want done to you. If you love, you will be loved; if you hate, you will be hated; if you judge, you will be judged; and if you accept all for what they are, you will be accepted for what you are.

Chapter 10

HEALTH

Health is life. It's nothing more and nothing less. Without the existence of diseases and pain in our bodies, we wouldn't even be aware of such thing as health, and we wouldn't even think of it to describe the state of the body without sickness. Without its opposite, health wouldn't even have its own name – it would just be life.

So why do we pray for health? Why do we desire health so much? Why do we seek it only when a pain in our body points out something broken? Isn't this then praying for life? Isn't it that we, in fact, desire more life in our body?

In other words, when our bodies start hurting, that is a sign of life leaving the body; it means that the mind occupies more of the body than You. The mind has pushed You away from the body, and now it manifests – in less life – in the body. A disease is nothing but a bad programming of the mind – like a virus in a computer.

So when we get sick, instead of bringing You back into the body, the mind takes our body to the doctor to patch it up because it doesn't have the knowledge to fix it itself. The mind is programmed to beat the heart and to breathe the air, but it can't fix the body when the programming is broken by negative thoughts because it doesn't know, and doesn't want to admit it either, that the thoughts, its programming, is the very cause of it. Throughout time, the minds of the world have studied diseases in people and compiled whole libraries of variants, solutions, and fixes. It's no wonder that in order to become a practitioner, people have to go through school for about twenty years of their life and still have to learn and keep up with the new discoveries – pretty much like Sisyphus' work.

Scientifically, it has been proven that 90% of illness and disease has its root cause in stress (NASD, n.d.). If you apply enough tension or stress on a chain, eventually one of the links will break. Similarly, in the body, if you apply enough tension or stress on it, eventually something will break.

Stress, in essence, is a cumulation of thoughts that aren't in harmony with life... with You. We will call them negative thoughts. As with every other thought in our mind, a negative thought has its own vibration, and on this vibration, it perceives similar thoughts. Think of it like the frequency of a radio – once tuned in to a station, you only hear what that station broadcasts. In the big picture, a negative thought brings about negative thoughts, which in turn bring about even more negative thoughts, and so on, until eventually the original thought is so deeply buried under the pile of negative thoughts that we can't even remember what it was about in the first place. And when you walk around with this pile of thoughts on a daily basis, you can imagine how much stress it puts on you, and that eventually your body will start becoming weaker.

Sometimes, we tell ourselves that all this weight makes us stronger. It's true, but only to the extent that we learn from it, move on, and leave it behind. Think of a bodybuilder – they go to the gym, lift some weights, their muscles become stronger, and so on, but have you ever seen a bodybuilder leaving the gym with the weights on their shoulders? No. They come back the next day for them, and in the meantime, they allow their body to recover.

Some believe that it's what we eat that makes our body unhealthy, though Jesus, some 2000 years ago, said, "What goes into someone's mouth does not defile them, but what comes out of their mouth, that is what defiles them." – Matthew 15:11 (The Holy Bible, 2011). The word is the result of a thought; therefore, the thought is what pollutes the body. Negative thoughts lead to an unhealthy body. Replace fearful thoughts with thoughts of love and joy and you keep life flowing through your body.

In Rhonda Byrne's (2006) phenomenal movie *The Secret*, Cathy Goodman comes on the screen to say that she cured her body from cancer with laughter and positive thoughts. For most people this seems like a joke; however, if we were to look into "why and how," we discover that laughter is a result of good feelings, relaxation, and a stress-free environment. Try to recall a moment when you were just before a very important meeting and you felt anxious and under stress; would you have been able to laugh if someone told you a joke? Now, think of the opposite; when you were happy and joyful but hit by some sad news, were you still able to laugh and be joyful?

Laughter relaxes the body, releases tension, and allows it to recover. It isn't a miracle that someone can cure cancer in their body on their own – it's natural! The root cause of cancer is stress and negative thoughts – remove those and the body recovers because life – You – will take over the body. By allowing You to live in a relaxed body, it only does what is natural for life to do – bring in more life.

I know a person who cared for her mother and her mother in law. Both, though not at the same time, were diagnosed with cancer and died. What kind of thoughts do you think a person can build in their mind when they have experienced how cancer eats life out of a body? She imagined herself living with cancer, and by doing that she created cancer in her own body, too. Now, she didn't see her life ending like that. She had good reasons to live longer, so she didn't give in and she didn't give up; her thoughts were now directed toward her two children and she saw herself looking after them – she imagined herself strong enough to raise them and eventually she cured her body of cancer.

Most people miss the key element when it comes to healing – **belief**. One has to believe that You can heal the body, or that a specific pill or treatment can heal it. Without belief in that something, there is no cure. Scientists work tirelessly to prove to the human minds how their treatments work in the body, and explain how the medication they administer to their patients helps the body to recover – this is but an attempt to make the minds of their patients **believe** in the cure because if one doesn't believe, or has no reason to live any longer, no treatment in the world can cure that person and it puts any treatment to shame.

The placebo effect is defined as a phenomenon in which some people experience a benefit after the administration of an inactive "look-alike" substance or treatment. This substance, or placebo, has no known medical effect. A placebo is a fake or sham treatment specifically designed without any active element. A placebo can be given in the form of a pill, injection, or even surgery. The classic example of a placebo is the sugar pill. Placebos are given to make patients **believe** they're getting a real treatment.

I mentioned previously about Dr. Joe Dispenza (2020) and his recovery story from the book *You Are the Placebo*. After the accident, the doctors concluded that his body was paralyzed and he would never be able to walk again, not even after a very complicated surgery. Those doctors' inability to **see** a way to fix his body was limited by their own bundle of knowledge – they had never seen or heard of anyone walking after that kind of diagnosis, but that wasn't Dr. Joe Dispenza's belief. He believed that there was a power within him that was bigger than his mind, and that it could heal and restore his body so it would function again, and within ten weeks, he walked out of the hospital.

From my personal experience, I can confirm that You and the mind can beat any treatment as long as they work together. When I was a student in a theological seminary studying the bible, we reached the part in which Jesus said: "Truly I tell you, if you have faith as small as a mustard seed, you can say to this mountain, 'Move from here to there,' and it will move. Nothing will be impossible for you" – Matthew 17:20 (The Holy Bible, 2011). That statement there got me thinking, and observing the world around me somehow confirmed it. I realized, to a very small degree, that even the belief in a lie can change someone's life, and I decided to change something I believed in – to test it.

Back in Romania, the winter season came along with colds and flu amongst people. One day I came up with a statement: "I never get the flu or a cold" – it was a lie, obviously, because every year up until then I had experienced the annoying symptoms of those viruses, but it became my new statement, and the more I said it, the more I started believing in it. A year passed by and I realized I'd not had symptoms of the flu or a cold – this only strengthened my belief because now I even had the proof. It was only when some people challenged my belief strongly, by bringing up memories from childhood, that my faith was shaken, and I would get symptoms of the flu occasionally, once in five years or so.

Now, when I look back, I know that only when the belief in my new lie was shaken, my body responded accordingly. It was my belief that was the cause of years of living in expectancy of catching the viruses, and after I changed my belief, I had years without any symptoms of the viruses. I'm not saying that I don't catch the viruses; all I'm saying is that the virus doesn't get to manifest more than a day before my body overpowers it. I confidently meet other people who have visible symptoms of a cold or flu, some even warn me not to get too close, but my conviction that I'm fine and I'll be alright, and my belief in my body's ability to heal superfast always works for me.

I also believe that there is an aura around me that literally protects me from viruses. Throughout the two years of the COVID-19 pandemic that preceded the writing of this book, I was out and about without the fear of being infected – I **knew** that I was protected, and even if I got the virus, my body would quickly eliminate it. I tested many times, mostly for traveling purposes, and I never had a positive result. I never had the virus, though I know for a fact I've been in contact with people who had symptoms of COVID-19, which was even confirmed with tests afterwards.

Our belief in our body's ability to overcome anything is the energy that fuels our cells to recovery. There is no disease that You can't overcome. Train your mind to believe whatever you want, and it will manifest that within your body, though if you allow your mind to create its own beliefs based on past experiences, that manifests also. My brother is afraid of drafts; he believes that by standing in drafty places he will get the flu – almost every time he gets it. My mother can't leave the house without her purse of pills – she believes she's sick and her only hope is within those blister packs. What our mind believes it manifests – choose your beliefs carefully, and change your beliefs if you must, but know that the cure to any disease, or sickness, is within your belief in your body's ability to heal.

There are people who get the flu or a cold every year, sometimes even the same month every year – their mind is programmed to expect it. Who programmed it? Sadly, each and every one of us does this unconsciously. When we were born, most of these programs were implanted into our minds by the closest people in our environment. I'm not saying that we should blame them because each and every one of us is responsible for our own lives, and we have the capacity to reprogram our mind at will – the way I did with mine – with a little white lie to trick the mind. Those close to us, who passed on their programming to us, also inherited or created this programming unconsciously, so we can't blame them for not being more careful with their life and we can't blame them for passing it on – that is their belief, their programming, and most probably, they never realized they have the ability to change it, but you do now, and you can change your beliefs, you can change your lifestyle, and you can improve your life. You know now that you have this ability because I just told you, and if you still choose to believe that it's impossible without giving it your best to prove it to yourself – that's on you.

I'm not saying that you should go and preach it to other people thinking you may risk making a fool of yourself, but I'm saying that your thoughts are your own. Whatever happens between You and your mind doesn't have to come out of your mouth; it can stay between You and your mind. You can teach your mind whatever you want, and you can repeat to your mind whatever statement you want, and nobody will know – they will only be able to see the end result.

Create yourself a set of positive affirmations and repeat those over and over to your mind, and eventually these affirmation will override the old beliefs and install new ones. Even those beliefs you already have are the results of some kind of affirmations; they're just not necessarily the kind you intentionally said to yourself but the kind you unconsciously did because you've heard them so many times from others.

For an affirmation to be effective in changing a belief to your liking, it has to be expressed in positive words that describe the end result in the present tense. "I don't want to get sick" is not as effective as "I am healthy." The mind works in images, and when you say the word "sick," a picture of it pops on the screen of your mind; when you say or think "healthy," a totally different image comes up. Using words that describe the end result helps your mind focus on the things you do want rather than the things you don't, and whatever the mind is focused on, it brings to the surface and commands your body to readjust so it can match the new belief.

It's the same with the tense you're using; when you state, "I want to be healthy," your mind unconsciously believes that you aren't healthy right now and it keeps manifesting in direct proportion to that belief, so in order to change your state, you have to change the belief. Changing the statement to "I am healthy" – despite appearances – forces the mind to "see" a different state and assume a new belief. What you see right now is the result of your old beliefs. Your new belief is "I am healthy," and results will start coming, so repeat that over and over – "I am healthy."

Remember that seeing is not believing; it's only the confirmation of your belief. For you to see one thing, you must have been believing it and its manifestation made it possible for you to see. **Believing is seeing**. Change your beliefs and your life changes. Create a set of simple affirmations that you can repeat over and over to your mind to reprogram it, like the one we mentioned before. "I am healthy," "I breathe in health," "Health flows through my veins," "I heal my body fast and easy," "I have a clean and healthy body," etc.

Do the same with any aspect of your life that you wish to change. Whatever it is that you see right now is a direct response of the beliefs impregnated in your mind. Consistently repeating affirmations of what you want to see in your life will change the beliefs of your mind. As you slowly adopt the new belief, the manifestation of that belief starts showing itself in your life.

Chapter 11

SHOW ME THE MONEY

Another essential part of life – and one that the world focuses on more and more these days – is the gathering of riches. Wanting more from life is only natural. We only have a limited time on this earth, and experiencing as much as possible is the least we can expect. We all desire, to some degree, a cozy home, a comfortable bed, a beautiful view, the ability to travel at will all over the world, to drive a comfortable car, wear beautiful clothes, eat delicious foods, and so on. In the world we live in right now – for our mind – money is essential to obtain all of these.

I'm sure that anyone, if they put their mind to it, can build a bed, a house, or a car, can create their own clothes, travel wherever they wish, or cook their own delicious foods without the need of a single coin, but what they have to give, in exchange for it, is the time they have, so in order for us to enjoy more things in life, money was created as means of exchange.

Thousands of years ago, humans were building their own homes, cooking their own meals, and creating their own "designer" clothes, but that was limited to their own knowledge and ability. Some people discovered different foods, while others discovered different clothes, and they decided to exchange items. In other terms, they were exchanging the time and ability to create a product with the time and ability of another. One became good at growing vegetables, while another became good at making clothes.

When the one making clothes became really good at it, more and more people would come to exchange their products, but the foods they received started going bad because they couldn't eat as much as they received in exchange for the clothes; meanwhile others needed the clothes but their crop wasn't ripe yet, and so the necessity for a later payment filled their lives. So they started giving each other promissory notes to be paid at a later time.

In short, this is an idea of the way the necessity for money came into the life of humans – a promise to be paid at a later time for the services provided. If you take a bill released in England and look at it, you'll find this written on it: "I promise to pay the bearer on demand the sum of [...] pounds," a promise made by the Bank of England. A bill released in Scotland says, "Bank of Scotland plc promises to pay to the Bearer on demand [...] pounds sterling at its registered office, Edinburgh." In Australia it says, "This Australian note is legal tender throughout Australia and its territories." In the United States it says, "This note is legal tender for all debts, public and private."

The point is that money is but promises for payments on demand – they have no value! The real value is the service that's been offered in exchange for the note of promise. When we wish for money but have nothing to give in exchange, we are only beggars at the mercy of someone else.

So as the real value of money is within the service provided, if you want more money, you have to offer more and a better service. The more you provide, the more promises you get; the better the quality of your service, the bigger the promises. When people demand more promises for less, or worse quality for their service, the value decreases, and the value of the promise is reduced, and that's how economies collapse – too many promises that have wobbly foundations or that haven't been kept.

When my wife and I bought our first home, we didn't have enough promises gathered to pay for it, so we asked the bank if they were willing to help us pay for our new home, and we promised that we would render services that would cover the cost and we'd pay the amount back in time (with interest, obviously).

Because we had only one percent of the value of the house, I did two things to increase the flow of money so we could gather the necessary deposit: 1) I became better at what I did, and 2) I dedicated more of my time to what I did best. Within a few months, our accounts were flooded with "promises", and we moved in swiftly.

"Money is a reward received for service rendered," said Bob Proctor, "The amount of money you earn is always in direct ratio to need for what you do, your ability to do it, and the difficulty there is in replacing you. When you become really good at what you're doing, you'll become very difficult to replace. Want to earn a lot of money? Fall in love with what you do and get better at it."

Wherever you are, there is a need for what you do. Most people misunderstand this concept as they define themselves through what they've studied in school, by their diploma, or by their experience in doing a particular thing. You can study anything you want; you can get any diploma you want, and by starting small you can get the experience also.

Wherever you are, there is a need for you because you have this amazing computer that we call the brain, which is capable of learning and relearning on demand. You can learn anything, and you can do anything you want, regardless of where you are on the planet, the diploma you have, or the experience you've accumulated. You can start anywhere, learn anything, and if you become passionate about it, you get better at it. The better you get at what you do, the more you will be paid for the thing you're doing.

The only thing that stops you from doing anything is you. Think about it! When someone suggests a new job, do you take it and figure out later how to do it, or you say, "I'm not very good at that." Whatever you do, it's your choice. You decide if your knowledge is the limit to what you can do, or whether you are willing to gather more knowledge to learn more so you can earn more. Richard Branson, founder of Virgin Group, said, "If someone offers you an amazing opportunity and you're not sure you can do it, say YES, then learn how to do it later." I believe he knows what he's talking about as he built an empire on this philosophy.

There is this fear of starting over that holds people back. You never start over! Nobody will ever take away your knowledge when you learn something new; it's not like some sort of memory disk that you replace, and it's not like you have limited memory and you have to clear whatever you have saved in your mind to make space for the new information. Your mind may be attached and comfortable to the thing you've done for so long, but that's not Your limitation.

When you learn something new, you add to your existing knowledge and you can even develop a different perspective. The Wright brothers weren't aviation engineers, but that didn't stop them from learning how to build and fly a plane – they used their existing knowledge and imagination to create something new.

Your past experiences may define what you are today, but that should never be the limit of what you can do. What you are today may be the result of your past thoughts and decisions, but that doesn't have to be your future also. Because today – right now – you can decide to change that future, and you can decide to learn something new to add to your existing experience and create something unique. There is no one person like you, and you can use this in any field you want to pursue.

My suggestion is to start right where you are. If you already have a job or business, become better every day at that job or business; always put your mind to look for ways in which you can improve yourself – you don't have to be better than anyone else, but you have to get better than your old self. If you only strive to be better by one percent per day, in a year you'll be thirty-seven times that. Your income may not seem to grow that higher, but your value surely does. Keep at it and the income will follow.

If on the other hand, you're "in between jobs," don't stay "in between" just because you think you're worth more than what is on the market or be afraid you'll sell yourself short. If you are indeed worth more, you'll be able to prove it shortly enough, and you will be given the opportunity. A very good friend of mine went to an interview for a job at the bottom of the ladder. During the interview, the employer proposed to him another job at a higher pay because they saw in him higher potential – go for whatever job and become better at it; he became so good at his job that soon he was offered a management position.

Go for the company you want to prosper in, take whatever job they have to offer, and get really good at it. You won't stay there for long because when you do more and become better, you overflow the space you're occupying, and another position must be offered to you. When you become valuable to the company, they will want to keep you there.

So when you want a raise, don't go asking your boss for it, and don't compete with others for a position, simply become better at what you do, not with the purpose of showing your boss you are better but with the purpose of increasing your own value, and a position will be created for you. If the company you work for doesn't appreciate you, another company will do and will come to offer you a better paid job.

The ultimate goal, though, should be to do whatever you are passionate about. Working for a company should only be a step toward your passion. Use the spare time you have outside your job to do what you love and you are passionate about. Become better at it every day, and eventually you will be able to share your value with the world and be paid accordingly.

Up until about two hundred years ago there weren't many employees; people were entrepreneurs: they learned a trade, became good at it, and earned a living out of it. Whether they were shoemakers, builders, tailors, merchants, or artists, they all found a market for their value.

When the era of mass production came upon the world, companies needed workforce, so they came up with monthly (or weekly) wages, secure income, and paid leave. This became so attractive that everyone wanted to work for a company, and some were so proud that they made their kids wish for the same – a new generation was born. Opportunities to get paid within a month or a week, without investment other than one's time and ability, to follow simple tasks.

But the times change. We are now past the era of manual labor; we have machines and computers that are doing most of these tasks for companies, and soon all workforces will be replaced by robots. If you want to strive, you have to ride with the tide and not against it.

Observe the world and you will find opportunities for prosperity everywhere there is a link missing. Where there are problems, there are opportunities, and where there is shortage, there is opportunity. Dr. Joe Vitale told a story in his book, The Secret to Attracting Money, about how he once went out with his friends and they all ordered Margaritas, and because he was doing bodybuilding at the time and had to watch his weight, he had to limit the caloric intake and couldn't order himself a Margarita because it had way too many calories. He thought that it would be nice if there was a Margarita for athletes with less calories – there was the idea! He really thought about it, and he went to Marcus Gitterle, M.D., a product creator; and Jeff Sargent, a former health food store owner, and asked them to create a margarita mix with no sugar. They created Fit-a-Rita, which is now sold all over Latin America.

> You must get rid of the thought of competition. You are to create, not to compete for what is already created.
>
> You do not have to take anything away from anyone.
>
> You do not have to drive sharp bargains.
>
> You do not have to cheat, or to take advantage. You do not need to let any man work for you for less than he earns.
>
> You do not have to covet the property of others, or to look at it with wishful eyes; no man has anything of which you cannot have the like, and that without taking what he has away from him.
>
> You are to become a creator, not a competitor; you are going to get what you want, but in such a way that when you get it every other man will have more than he has now. (Wattles, 2014)

The thought of competition belongs to the mind. In its limited ability, the mind can't comprehend the idea of creation; it thinks only in terms of what is – as if that's all there will ever be – and in order for one to have money or anything else, that one will have to take it from someone else. You, on the other hand, have no limitation; You creates over and over all the things that You want to experience in this life, without the need to take it away from someone else, because You is in everyone else, and taking something from someone is similar to taking from yourself.

Money is energy. The value that goes with money is the energy in the form of the work of those who gave their time and energy to create that value manifested in the paper that is the symbol of a promise of exchange. When one takes without giving or takes more than the value of the service provided, they're inflating their own energy, which eventually will burst out. This may not necessarily mean that they'll lose the money, though we've seen so many people going bankrupt, but it may be the energy of health in their body, or the energy in their relationships with others.

When You create, you expand, and in so doing you create a void within to be filled with energy; therefore, the energy will be drawn to you. Whether in the form of money, health, love, or relationships, the space you created must be filled, and it will be filled according to your focus. If your focus is on money, you will attract money in direct proportion to the number of people who have received an increase through the value of your creation. The more people who receive an increase of energy through your creation, the more energy in the form of money will come to you.

So when your value adds to the life of another person, you will have expanded to the size of one person. If your creation influences in a positive way the life of many people, you will have expanded to the size of all those people. Whether you're an artist, entertainer, writer, inventor, farmer, computer programmer, etc., the number of people influenced by your produce decides the size to which you expand, which in turn attracts the energy correspondent to your creation.

The same applies when giving. When you give energy in the form of money, you receive energy in the form of goods in exchange. When you give energy in the form of service, you receive energy in the form of money. When you give energy in the form of help, whether it's money, a helping hand, precious advice, or a shoulder for one in need, you create a void to be filled. Now here is the trick! If you expect the energy to come from the same source you've given it to, or if your focus is on that particular source, you block all the other sources. But if you give without expecting it back from the same source, you allow yourself to be filled with energy from all sources.

Charities are the clearest example of this; some even call it a law for the precision with which it works – the law of vacuum, the law of giving, or the law of receiving – it doesn't have a specific name or definition as our mind doesn't yet has the capacity to comprehend its entire functionality and its extent. A charity, as an organization, has at its core the aim of influencing the lives of people in a positive way. The more people they influence, the bigger the charity grows. The same applies to a charitable person – the more a person gives and influences the lives of other people, the more they expand.

A classic example is Percy Ross, a self-made millionaire, who, after he sold his business for $8,000,000, split the money four ways among himself, his wife, and his two sons, and then he decided to give away his share. He had a column in a newspaper called Thanks a Million, and through this, he'd send money to people who would write in with requests. The column ran in over 800 publications for seventeen years, but the impressive thing is that, though he only started giving from his share of $2,000,000, he ended up giving away over $20,000,000.

The richest people give the most to charitable causes, and most of us believe that they give because they have. The truth is that **they have**

because they give, and the more they give, the more they get. One of the rules of rich people is that the first ten percent of their earnings goes to charity. Whether inspired by the legendary book *The Richest Man in Babylon* by George S. Clason or they have learned it from other rich people, this rule – this law – is the pump that makes the money flow.

What you focus your mind on expands, and gratitude is the most powerful tool for focus. The more you are grateful for what you have, the more what you focus on expands. If your focus is on money and you are grateful for all that you have, your money grows. If your focus is on lack of money and you can't even be grateful for the little that you have, your money doesn't grow.

So how do you focus on money when you don't have enough? That's actually quite simple. No matter how little comes through your hands, put aside ten percent – in a savings account or something similar. It may seem not much in the beginning, but if you keep at it with perseverance, in ten weeks you'll have the equivalent of another week's pay, or in ten months you'll have another month's pay. As you look at it, every time you are grateful for that little that you have, you create a ripple in the universe, which moves itself into returning more. In the same manner that you barely notice putting aside the ten percent, you will barely notice how your income grows, and ten months later you won't only have an extra month's pay but you will have had a pay rise or a bonus as well.

The secret to this is in growing your mind, educating it, and transforming it into a money magnet. Did you know that about seventy percent of lottery winners were broke within five years of cashing their ticket? Their mind wasn't a strong enough magnet to keep hold of that much money. The other thirty percent were usually people who already had dealings with large amounts of money in the past and their mind was trained to keep it and/or multiply it. I have even read about a couple who won the lottery twice and a few years later were living on social benefits. Their desire to become rich overnight was strong enough to manifest it, but their mind wasn't ready to hold on to and manage that amount of money.

Getting rich overnight isn't the solution to an abundant life. Growing a rich mind ensures a continuous flow of money – even in "unforeseen circumstances." There are countless examples of people who have grown a rich mind and their life grew rich as a result also. Some people, due to unforeseen circumstances, have become broke, but only in physical riches – they've lost their fortunes, but not their minds, and shortly after, they've managed to create a new fortune much faster than the previous one because their mind was trained to think rich. Examples like this are Abraham Lincoln, Walt Disney, Elton John, Larry King and many more. In most cases, the cause was poor management, but that didn't decrease the actual value they had built over the years, and no one could take their mind from them either. The real fortune isn't in the bank account; it's in the mind because the mind is your most trustworthy companion on this earth – train it well and it will support You well.

The expression "The rich get richer, and the poor get poorer" is true because of people's mindset. As recorded in the Christian bible (The Holy Bible, 2011; Matthew 25:29), Jesus said, "Whoever has will be given more, and they will have an abundance. Whoever does not have, even what they have will be taken from them." It sounds like a cruel statement, and most people ignore it because they don't understand it. The statement refers to the power of our mind to multiply the seeds – ideas or money – that we plant in it, or to lose all the seeds that we don't: "Whoever has **seeds planted** will be given more, and they will have an abundance. Whoever does not have **seeds planted**, even what they have will be taken from them."

According to Rhonda Byrne (2012), in her book *The Magic*, this text is missing a different word – gratitude. "Whoever has **gratitude** will be given more, and they will have an abundance. Whoever does not have **gratitude**, even what they have will be taken from them." I'd go on to say that "gratitude" could also be replaced with love, joy, happiness, or even stress, hate, jealousy, and so on. Whatever feeling you may have, you will be given more, and you will have an abundance; whatever feeling you abandon, even what you have left will be taken from you. Abandon the seeds that you don't want and plant the seeds that you do want.

Robert A. Russel (2016), in his book *You Too, Can Be Prosperous*, said, "For he that hath the Consciousness of Spiritual Substance, to him shall be given, and he that hath not the Consciousness of Universal Substance, from him shall be taken even that which he hath. The more conscious you are of this Universal Substance, the more it will work for you, and the richer you will become."

If you grow seeds of money in your mind, you will have an abundance. A savings account in which, every time you are paid for a service, you deposit ten percent will show you how your worth is growing over time. It will grow your confidence in your ability to grow rich; it will help you make decisions in favor of your happiness. If you're employed somewhere that no longer resonates with your values, you will have the necessary backup to make the decision to leave and find a workplace that suits your vibration; if you're in a position to make a financial decision, you will be backed by your savings account – the bigger the account, the stronger your confidence and ability to make bigger decisions.

I heard a story about a young CEO who was going through financial difficulties. One day she went to the park near her office to clear her mind. Next to her, on the bench, an old man sat to rest as well. He looked at her, sensed her distress, and asked what was troubling her. She explained how her company was going through a difficult financial situation, and if she had just $500,000, she'd be able to fix the problem, and save the company and the jobs of her employees. The old man took out a check book, wrote a check for $500,000, and handed it to her while saying that he expected the money back in one year. Filled with joy and gratitude, she headed back to her office, put the check in the safe, and started working on the solution. Within a few months, not only did she save her company but she did that without even cashing the check. Her confidence grew so strong that she was able to negotiate new terms with her suppliers, make better decisions, and act on those that she was fearful about.

One year later she went back to the park to meet the old man on the same bench as agreed. The old man showed up as expected and she handed him the same check back that she received a year before, and told him how grateful she was for his help and how his goodness helped her save and grow her company. Their conversation was suddenly interrupted by a nurse, who exclaimed, "Here you are. Let's get you back!" She then turned around toward the young CEO and said, "He always runs away from the care home to talk to people, pretending to be John D. Rockefeller." (Canfield, 2012)

There are three points that need to be underlined in this story: 1) she never needed the money to save her company, 2) her confidence played the biggest role in saving the company, and 3) her faith in the back-up check was enough. Once you have the back-up savings, your confidence will go up and you will discover that things become possible when you aren't under the pressure of lack of money. The idea of this savings account isn't for you to dip your fingers in it every time you want a new pair of shoes, the latest mobile phone, or to go on vacation.

The idea of it is to constantly grow it by adding ten percent to expand your money consciousness and only use it if everything else fails. If it hasn't failed, there is no need to use it. There is always another way, and there is always a solution to any problem; keep looking for it, and if everything fails and you have to use part of it, think of it as a loan that you have to pay back, and increase the amount you pay into your savings account to twenty percent, if you can't afford to put it back all at once, until you have restored the amount you've used.

Your money consciousness is directly related to the amount of money that you see in your bank accounts – it grows as your bank accounts grow. If you can think of money, you can attract money, but you can't keep money if you don't have a money consciousness equal to the fortune you want to spend. Think of your savings account as the money pipe – the bigger the account, the bigger the flow.

If, right now, you are employed and your wage comes as a fixed amount every week or every month, you may be thinking of setting up a standing order and having the funds transferred automatically on payday. That is a great approach, but what is even greater is to do this manually every time. This way you get to see the money that came into your account and to feel gratitude for it, you get to make the transfer and be grateful for it, and then see your savings account and be grateful for it – feel as much gratitude for the money that flows through your accounts as you can because the energy of gratitude will both expand your money consciousness and attract ideas and opportunities from the "Universal Intelligence" for you to make even more money.

Money is "thought energy" manifested. The more you think about the abundance of money, the more you manifest. When we think that money can only come from one source, our employer or the business we run, we limit the flow of money to that one source. To quote Bob Proctor: "Money doesn't come from your workplace but through it." When you think that for you to get more money it means to get a promotion, a bonus, or a better paid job, you limit your opportunities because the universe responds to all your thoughts, and if you only see, on the screen of your mind, money coming to you from your job, your growth will be limited by what your employer can afford to pay you. At the end of the day, you can't impose your wish on other people, and you must have a creative mind in such a way that when you get a wage increase, everybody else gets an increase also. If your promotion means for you to go after someone else's position, you have dropped from the creative plane to the competitive one. That person may not be suited for the position that they just lost, but your gain is someone else's loss.

If you love your job that much, and you love your employer so much that you want to stay there for as long as possible, think of abundance for the whole company, think of an increase for all your colleagues, and think of bonuses for everybody. When the company grows thanks to your creative contribution, a new position will be created for you, and this way you will have made room for another to take your position, and in this way everybody wins.

But my argument, when it comes to thoughts of abundance, is to not limit the source of money to one but to expand it and imagine that money may come from everywhere and is literally growing on trees. This way you allow your mind to expand and find opportunities at every corner. Everywhere you look you will see another way of making money.

You are the money because you are the value that creates the money. The people you serve in one way or multiple ways will bring the money to you. Become a person of value, of help, and support. Create opportunities for others to earn, and when they earn, you earn; when they're enriched by the value You gave them, you are enriched. The more You give, the more you receive.

Chapter 12

THE I IN YOU

I am everything. I am all that exists. The non-physical world is a collection of thoughts. The physical world that You live in is simply a projection of each of those thoughts. Everything that You see, feel, hear, taste, and smell in the physical world has been created by my thoughts. You are a projection of an almost infinite number of thoughts. Each time you have any thought, it begins in the non-physical world and it is projected into the physical. What you call your consciousness exists in the non-physical and is projected into what seems like a real physical world to you. I am constantly projecting all the thoughts of billions of people into the physical world. I am each of You. Your thoughts are mine. There is no separation. You are God. (Werley, 2020)

We are all one. We are the same. We are You. I'm You, and you are me. When I love You, I love myself. When I hate You, I hate myself. When I love me, I love You. When I hate me, I hate You. "Truly I tell you, whatever you did for one of the least of these brothers and sisters of mine, you did for me." – Matthew 25:40 (The Holy Bible, 2011). "Holding on to anger is like grasping a hot coal with the intent of throwing it at someone else; you are the one who gets burned," said Buddha. Enlightened people throughout the ages have realized this truth, and it's been with us all along.

When we identify with our mind and body, we lose our true nature, and we lose our true identity – the energy there is in all and through all. We lose ourselves to the limitations of our body and mind, and we imprison ourselves within it. If you think of yourself as "only human," you can't be something else – that's what you are because You think of yourself as a body.

> Enlightenment is nothing but realizing, understanding the truth that you are the beingness behind all of this. Come to know that you are not a person but are the feeling of beingness that you feel before anything else every morning. You don't think, but you are. Thinking happens on you, doing happens inside of you, but you are this space that it all happens within. Space does not think, but space has a component that

the mind inside of the body can feel as a personal I. All you need to do is understand this is what is happening. That is where I comes from, the mental interpretation of what consciousness experiences when it comes into contact with the beingness behind all. Contemplate this and see this truth for yourself. Feel where I arises, then look at the beingness that exists behind the mental label the mind gives it. Feel the I before it becomes I. Feel it as the beingness, the existing that it is. Nothing more, nothing less, just being. Know that this feeling is you. That's all. It is you, it is me, it is everyone else reading these same words today, tomorrow, ten years from now, it is all the same me, right now. That which I am knows no time, no space, but it is eternally right here, now. Feel yourself, don't give yourself more attributes. Feel the feeling of beingness. (Wright, 2014)

Thought is what you are; thought is your existence. One thought is sufficient to express the I in and through your body. **I am** ... Whatever comes after this is pure manifestation. The life I live right now is a perfect match of all my **I am** thoughts. The life you live right now is a perfect match of all of your **I am** thoughts. The life we all live on this planet is a perfect match of all of our **I am** thoughts. The God who's ruling the world is You. You are the creator and the destroyer of all the things of this world. That deity to which, sometimes, we fall on our knees to pray to, lives within you, not above in the sky but within every single breath you take, every sip of water, every drop of blood that flows through your body, every one of the trillions of cells that constitute your body, every tear, and every smile.

There may be a god who created the universe, but You are the god who creates Your Own Universe. Joy, love, abundance, and prosperity become what You are when you say **I am** ... I am joy. I am love. I am abundance. I am prosperity.

I am sad, I am single, I am poor, I am sick, and I am broken – they're equal manifestations of the same **I am** ...

You are what you say you are. In our minds we tend to believe that we are merely stating some conclusions. "I am hurt" isn't a consequence of some sort of event that happened in our life that made us feel hurt. That event didn't hurt you; your statement did, and you chose to be hurt as a consequence of that event. Instead, you could choose to ignore the event or even laugh as a consequence of the same event. Think about it! If something falls on your hand while working, you may feel hurt as a consequence. If the same thing fell on your hand while doing something that you're passionate about, you may be so focused on your passion that you ignore it completely. If the

YOU and Your Own Universe

same thing fell on your hand while playing with your friends, you may even laugh at the situation.

> The word is creative, as Emmet Fox says, and the strongest and most creative word is I Am. Whenever you say I Am, you are calling upon the universe to do something for you, and it will do it. Whenever you say I Am, you are drawing a check upon the universe, it will be honored and cashed sooner or later, and the proceeds will go to you. If you say I am tired, sick, poor, fed up, disappointed, getting old, then you are drawing checks for future trouble and limitations. When you say I am Divine Life, I am Divine Truth, I am Divine Freedom, I am Divine Substance, I am Eternal Substance, you are drawing a check on the bank of heaven and surely that check will be honored with health and plenty for you. (Russell, 2016)

How we react to the circumstances in our lives is entirely up to us. We always choose the reaction. It may not feel like a choice when we unconsciously train our mind to react in a specific way to certain events, but that can be changed. You are what you choose to be. You are what your **I am** statement is.

Rich people think rich thoughts, sick people think sick thoughts, poor people think poor thoughts, and happy people think happy thoughts. The dominant thoughts in one's mind manifest in their life. You may be poor and have a rich thought and you may win some money on a scratch card – that doesn't make you rich. But consistently thinking rich thoughts, despite the current circumstances, will certainly make you rich. You may be a healthy person and have a thought about sickness. That thought may manifest as a flu – that doesn't make you sick, but consistently thinking sick thoughts, despite you having a healthy body overall, will make you sick.

Gratitude is one of the best forms of manifestation of whatever you want in your life. Focusing on the things that you have and what you are creates similar thoughts in your mind; therefore, manifesting them in your life. Affirmations have the same effect – they inundate your mind with the nature of the thoughts you constantly affirm.

We are the same energy. We are one in nature, but we are different in creation. The way we train our mind, or allow our mind to be trained, makes a difference in manifestation between each and every individual. That's why we are all unique in manifestation – it's impossible for two minds to have exactly the same thoughts throughout a whole life, but it isn't impossible for two minds to have similar thoughts if they're inspired by the same mission.

Today we find this very often in sport competitions where all the team players, while in the game, have the same mission; each one individually plays their role, but as a whole, they have the same dominant thought. Winning, therefore, isn't a matter of ability but of mindset.

If you want the world to change, you have to plant in its mind thoughts which reflect that change. Pictures of sickness raise awareness, but they don't fix the sickness. Pictures of melting ice at the poles raise awareness, but they don't stop the ice from melting. If you want health in the world, show pictures of health, raise awareness about health, and plant thoughts of health in the minds of the people. If you want to protect the planet, show its beauty, appreciate its value, and plant pictures of beautiful nature in the minds of the people.

What we collectively think, we manifest. From the mind's perspective, we tend to blame others for the things that are "out of our control." We can't take responsibility for the wars that others initiated, we can't take responsibility for terrorist attacks, and we can't take responsibility for pandemics or for climate changes. Our mind's opinion is that we don't have enough power to influence any of them, and it's the government's responsibility to look after all these things. Then when they happen, we blame the government for not doing a better job – that's simply how the mind works in its limitation.

What is the government made of? People, right? How did these people get to be there? Some studied and worked hard to make a difference for us all, while others have been elected by the majority of people because they shared with us their dream – their vision – of a better world, and we believed in it, but they're still people like you and me. How do they make a difference? In their own way; by engaging each and every one of us to act differently because, like Albert Einstein said, "Doing the same thing over and over and expecting different results is insanity," so we must do things differently if we want different results. We – each and every one of us.

Every single action that each and every one of us takes in the direction of change counts. Every decision that we take makes a difference, like a little stone thrown in a still lake – it makes ripples in the water that reach the entire shore of the lake all the way around – it affects the whole lake. If you want to see change, you have to be the change. You have to be an example for those who don't know, and not by imposing your view on others, or by forcing others to do what you think is good, but by example.

There are dozens of people who made a difference in my life and who made me become a better person, and not one of them achieved this by forcing me or manipulating me into doing it – all of them set an example that I picked from them, and most have no clue they changed my life. If you take a moment to think about it, you'll discover similar people in your life. You'll realize most of your actions aren't yours, and most of the things you're doing are imitations of things you've admired in others. From the way you cut your hair, how you dress, or how you walk to the way you do the big things in life, some of them aren't your own – you've seen them in others. You chose those that were most suited to you and made them your own.

Regardless of whether you want it or not, you are an influencer also; you set an example for others too – it's up to you whether that example is a good one or not. Do you have children, nephews, or nieces? They're your biggest fans! Be that change for these people because they're the ones to carry on your legacy – they will remember the example you set and will carry it on throughout generations.

> You have no right to use your will power upon another person, even for his own good, for you do not know what is for his good [...] there is not the slightest necessity for doing so. Indeed, any attempt to use your will upon others will only tend to defeat your

purpose. You do not need to apply your will to things in order to compel them to come to you. [...] Substance is friendly to you and is more anxious to give you what you want than you are to get it. [...] When you know what to think and do, then you must use your will to compel yourself to think and do the right things – that is the legitimate use of the will in getting what you want, to use it in holding yourself to the right course. Use your will to keep yourself thinking and acting in a certain way. Do not try to project your will, or your thoughts or your mind out into space to act on things or people. Keep your mind at home. It can accomplish more there than elsewhere. (Wattles, 2014)

Controlling things and people by force is laborious and feels like swimming upstream in a river. Creating the circumstances by thought alone is like flowing with the river downstream. The universe knows all and sees all – using its power in your favor accomplishes more and faster. Employ the power of the universe through faith and know that it will deliver your vision in the fastest way possible. The mind's limitation can't see all the options available, so don't use your mind to figure out how you're going to accomplish what you want; leave this task to the mighty force of the universe, and surrender to its knowledge the same way you would trust a navigator to take you to a new destination.

You can do, be, and have anything you want. You now know how You can employ both the power of the mind and the power of the universe. Use them both wisely so You can explore and experience all that You want this time around on Earth. The world responds quicker to love and kindness, so use that to get where you want.

The Beginning of Your new life...

ACKNOWLEDGMENTS

This book is a result of the work of hundreds and thousands of people throughout history. Their work from the beginning of writings to this day has been reshaped and reformed in the light of new information discovered century by century. I have only built on the work of millions of people since the beginning of the world.

On the next page, in references, are mentioned the authors, programs, and books that served me as inspiration in the creation of this book, and to whom I am truly grateful from the bottom of my heart. Most of the authors have already been mentioned throughout the book, but all inspired me equally in reaching the fundamental conclusion described in it.

Although it goes without saying, I am truly grateful to my parents and my wife for helping me become the person I am today.

Deep gratitude to my mentor, Sheena Cantar, for she has managed to make the light in me shine brighter than ever.

Last, but not least, I am truly grateful to Victoria Seymour of SEYMOUR PROOFREADING, for the amazing service: proofreading and editing.

REFERENCES

Allen, J. (2020). *As A Man Thinketh*. Road 2 Success.
https://www.amazon.co.uk/As-Man-Thinketh-Classic-Character-ebook/dp/B07FB2JV8W

Bristol, C. (2019). *The Magic of Believing*. Digital Fire.
https://www.amazon.co.uk/gp/product/B07P39LF5T/

Bristol, C. (2015). TNT: It Rocks the Earth [Audiobook]. Retrieved from
https://www.amazon.co.uk/gp/product/B014JT0U2A/

Byrne, R. (2013). *Hero*. Simon & Schuster Ltd. Byrne, R. (2016). How The Secret Changed My Life [Audiobook]. Retrieved from
https://www.amazon.co.uk/gp/product/1471158195/

Byrne, R. (2020). *The Greatest Secret* [Audiobook]. Retrieved from
https://www.amazon.co.uk/gp/product/B08FTJLYRD/

Byrne, R. (2012). *The Magic*. Simon & Schuster Ltd.

Byrne, R. (2010). *The Power*. Retrieved from
https://www.amazon.co.uk/gp/product/0857201700/

Byrne, R. (2006). *The Secret*. Retrieved from
https://www.amazon.co.uk/gp/product/1847370292/

Canfield, J. (2014). *The Key to Living the Law of Attraction*. Retrieved from
https://www.amazon.co.uk/gp/product/1409151638/

Canfield, J. (2012). *The Success Principles* [Audiobook]. Retrieved from
https://www.amazon.co.uk/gp/product/B007ROEF62/

Clear, J. (2018). *Atomic Habits* [Audiobook]. Retrieved from https://www.amazon.co.uk/gp/product/1847941834/

Corey, C. (Director). (2020). *Superhuman: The Invisible Made Visible.* [TV Documentary]. Omnium Media; Omnium Media. https://www.superhumanfilm.com/

Covey, S. R. (2013). *The 7 Habits of Highly Effective People.* Retrieved from https://www.amazon.co.uk/Habits-Highly-Effective-People-Powerful-ebook/dp/B00GOZV3TM

Crum, Alia J., and Langer, Ellen J. (2007*). Mind-set matters: Exercise and the placebo effect.* Psychological Science 18, no. 2: 165-171. http://nrs.harvard.edu/urn-3:HUL.InstRepos:3196007

Dispenza, J. PhD. (2014). *Breaking the Habit of Being Yourself* [Audiobook]. Retrieved from https://www.amazon.co.uk/gp/product/B0868YNXR3/

Dispenza, J. PhD. (2020). *You Are the Placebo* [Audiobook]. Retrieved from https://www.amazon.co.uk/gp/product/1781802572/

Dooley, M. (2020). *A Beginner's Guide to the Universe.* Hay House UK Ltd.

Dooley, M. (2017). *Playing the Matrix* [Audiobook]. Retrieved from https://www.amazon.co.uk/gp/product/B073RR9TLG/

Emerson, R. W. (2017). *Self-Reliance and Other Essays.* AmazonClassics. https://www.amazon.co.uk/Self-Reliance-Other-Essays-AmazonClassics-Emerson-ebook/dp/B0752MV77R

FlightRadar24 (n.d.). *Live Air Traffic.* https://www.flightradar24.com/data/statistics

Goddard, N. (2015). *Feeling Is the Secret* [Audiobook]. Retrieved from https://www.amazon.co.uk/gp/product/B00ZGHC1IG/

Goddard, N. (2019). *The Power of Awareness* [Audiobook]. Retrieved from https://www.amazon.co.uk/gp/product/B07V1J1R9G/

Goddard, N. (2014). *Your Faith Is Your Fortune* [Audiobook]. Retrieved from https://www.amazon.co.uk/gp/product/B00LH09E2C/

Haanel, C. F. (2013). *The Master Key System*. Merchant Books.

Hill, N. (2020). *Success Through a Positive Mental Attitude*. DIGITAL FIRE (2nd edition). https://www.amazon.co.uk/gp/product/B089QL8DJ1/

Hill, N. (2013). *The Law of Success*. Sublime Books. https://www.amazon.co.uk/gp/product/B00DQIAAHQ/

Hill, N. (2007). *Think and Grow Rich* [Audiobook]. Retrieved from https://www.amazon.co.uk/gp/product/B002SQ3OIO/

Hill, N. (2014). *You Can Work Your Own Miracles* [Audiobook]. Retrieved from https://www.amazon.co.uk/gp/product/B00QI12DBY/

Kandler, M. (2019). *4 Brain Chemicals That Make You Happy*. Happyfeed. https://www.happyfeed.co/research/4-brain-chemicals-make-you-happy

Kellett, J. (2014). *The Human Body for Kids: 150+ Amazing Facts about the Human Body*. https://www.amazon.ca/Human-Body-Kids-Amazing-Facts-ebook/dp/B00HYNE3BI/

Kelly, M. (2004). *The Rhythm of Life*. Beacon Publishing.

Linguistic Society of America. (n.d.) *How many languages are there in the world?* https://www.linguisticsociety.org/content/how-many-languages-are-there-world

Maltz, M. PhD. (2017). *Psycho-Cybernetics* [Audiobook]. Retrieved from https://www.amazon.co.uk/gp/product/B06XRL8VXB/

Murphy, J. PhD. (2020). *The Power of Your Subconscious Mind*. Diamond Pocket Books (P) Ltd. https://www.amazon.co.uk/15-Minute-Read-Power-Subconscious-ebook/dp/B08541YNTW

NASD - National Ag Safety Database. (n.d.). *Stress Management for the Health of It*. https://nasdonline.org/1445/d001245/stress-management-for-the-health-of-it.html

Nightingale Conant Learning System. (2009). *The Richest Man in Babylon ... In Action* [Audiobook]. Retrieved from https://www.amazon.co.uk/gp/product/B00N4LI5S6/

Nightingale, E. (2019). *The Strangest Secret*. Reading Essentials. https://www.amazon.co.uk/Strangest-Secret-Earl-Nightingale-ebook/dp/B07SN86BJ7

OneKindPlanet. (n.d.). *Top 10 Strongest Animals*. https://onekindplanet.org/top-10/top-10-list-of-the-worlds-strongest-animals

Proctor, B. (2016). *The 7 Power Principles for Success* [Audiobook]. Retrieved from https://www.amazon.co.uk/7-Power-Principles-Success/dp/B01AO4RFJU

Proctor, B. (n.d.). *Thinking into Results*. A Proctor Gallagher Institute Program. Mentor: Sheena Cantar. https://sheena-cantar.mykajabi.com/Thinking%20Into%20Results

Proctor, B. (2015). *You Were Born Rich* [Audiobook]. Retrieved from https://www.amazon.co.uk/You-Were-Born-Rich/dp/B0187M5WDW

Proctor, B., Canfield, J., Assaraf, J., Nichols, L. (2007). *Teachers of The Secret* [Audiobook]. Retrieved from https://www.amazon.co.uk/Teachers-Secret-Recorded-Live/dp/B002SQDEUC

Proctor, B., Widener, C., Allen, D., Iverson, L., Jett, P., Ingram, S. R. (2016). *The Mindset of a Millionaire* [Audiobook]. Retrieved from https://www.amazon.co.uk/Mindset-Millionaire-Success-Magnetism-Collection/dp/B01MTLBRED

Proctor, B., Widener, C., Iverson, L., Stack, L., Brown, L., Wieder, M., Sanborn, M., Bethel, S. M., Ziglar, Z. (2016). *Thinking Big* [Audiobook]. Retrieved from https://www.amazon.co.uk/Thinking-Big-Achieving-Greatness-Thought/dp/B01MDVNGIH

Quora. (2019). *Why did Albert Einstein reject the existence of time?* https://www.quora.com/Why-did-Albert-Einstein-reject-the-existence-of-time/answer/Paul-Mainwood

Quotes. (n.d.). Goodreads. https://www.goodreads.com/quotes

Quotes by Author. (n.d.). AZ Quotes. https://www.azquotes.com/

Radhe, K. (n.d.). *Ihaleakala Hew Len PhD. And Ho`Oponopono. Dr. Len's Amazing Success with Ho`Oponopono*. Blue Bottle Love. https://bluebottlelove.com/hew-len-hooponopono/

Robbins, T. (2020). *Unleash the Power Within* [Audiobook]. Retrieved from https://www.amazon.co.uk/Unleash-Power-Within-Personal-Transform/dp/B08562DCT8

Russel, R. A. (2016). *You Too, Can Be Prosperous* [Audiobook]. Retrieved from https://www.amazon.co.uk/You-Too-Can-Be-Prosperous/dp/B01N1F92CI

Schwartz, D. J. PhD. (2015). *The Magic of Thinking Big* [Audiobook]. Retrieved from https://www.amazon.co.uk/The-Magic-of-Thinking-Big/dp/B015EXTAEO

Svetasvatara Upanishad. (2008). YouSigma. https://www.yousigma.com/religionandphilosophy/sveta svatara.html

The Holy Bible. (2011). New International Version. https://www.bible.com/en-GB/

Physics Classroom. (n.d.). *Light Waves and Color - Lesson 2 - Color and Vision: The Electromagnetic and Visible Spectra.* https://www.physicsclassroom.com/class/light/Lesson-2/The-Electromagnetic-and-Visible-Spectra

Tolle, E. (2009). *A New Earth*. Penguin. https://www.amazon.co.uk/New-Earth-LIFE-CHANGING-otherworldly-Breakfast-ebook/dp/B002RI97IY

Tolle, E. (2000). *The Power of Now* [Audiobook]. Retrieved from https://www.amazon.co.uk/The-Power-of-Now/dp/B002SQ7HVO

Vitale, J. PhD. (2010). *The Abundance Paradigm* [Audiobook]. Retrieved from https://www.amazon.co.uk/Abundance-Paradigm-Moving-Attraction-Creation/dp/B00N4LI2NO

Vitale, J. PhD. (2014). *The Secret to Attracting Money* [Audiobook]. Retrieved from https://www.amazon.co.uk/The-Secret-to-Attracting-Money/dp/B00NN8IWMO

Walsch, N. D. (2018). *The Complete Conversations with God: An Uncommon Dialogue: Books I, II & III* [Audiobook]. Retrieved from https://www.amazon.co.uk/Complete-Conversations-God-Uncommon-Dialogue/dp/B07HB6Y56V

Walsch, N. D. (2010). *When Everything Changes, Change Everything*. Hodder & Stoughton. https://www.amazon.co.uk/When-Everything-Changes-Change-turmoil-ebook/dp/B003OICGDE

Wattles, W. D. (2014). *The Science of Getting Rich* [Audiobook]. Retrieved from https://www.amazon.co.uk/The-Science-of-Getting-Rich/dp/B00J61BX82

Werley, E. (2020). *One Truth, One Law: I AM, I Create* [Audiobook]. Retrieved from https://www.amazon.co.uk/One-Truth-Law-Am-Create/dp/B084Q43DCY

Wikipedia. (n.d.). https://en.wikipedia.org

Worldometer. (n.d.). *Car production*. https://www.worldometers.info/cars/

Wright, G. T. (2014). *How to Become Enlightened in 12 Days*. Retrieved from https://www.amazon.co.uk/How-Become-Enlightened-Days-Realization-ebook/dp/B00JM6R90C

If you would like to learn more about
Silviu Pristavu and his work, please visit:

www.arenes.pro

or write to:

silviu@arenes.pro

Printed in Great Britain
by Amazon

87270406R00153